W. DAYTON ROBERTS

REVOLUTION IN EVANGELISM

THE STORY OF EVANGELISM-IN-DEPTH
IN LATIN AMERICA

FOREWORD BY LEIGHTON FORD

MOODY PRESS • CHICAGO

To Jacob Stam and his fellow "Greathearts"
of the Latin America Mission's Board of Trustees
this book is dedicated
with affection and respect

CONTENTS

CHAPTER   PAGE

      FOREWORD   5

      PREFACE   8

1   *He Left a Team*   13

2   *Frustration, Failure*   21

3   *Reflection, Hope*   29

4   *First Experiment*   38

5   *Not Without Honor*   49

6   *Spotlight on Guatemala*   56

7   *To the Ends of the Earth*   65

8   *Slings and Arrows*   78

9   *Rethinking Evangelism—Evangelism-in-Depth Principles*   94

10   *Right Side Up—Evangelism-in-Depth Program*   111

      EPILOGUE   125

FOREWORD

THE WORLD is being convulsed. More fantastic changes have been taking place in the last two decades than in all previous history. Population is exploding. Transportation is shrinking the world. Knowledge is doubling every ten years. Nations are striving to take their places under the sun. And mankind is haunted by the specter of possible annihilation.

For all these changes, as the French proverb says, "The more things change, the more they are the same." There still remains the need for the deepest revolution —the change of man's heart. I recall asking a South American newspaper editor if President Kennedy's Alliance for Progress would work in his country. He replied that if there could be a change of attitude on the part of the landowners, of the ordinary people and of the government, then it would work. In other words, their deepest need was a spiritual revolution on every level of society.

The gospel of Jesus Christ provides this revolutionary power. But the gospel calls for more than an opinion. It calls for action. What is needed is not just for Christians to be spectators of this revolution, but

5

something is needed that will galvanize them into revolutionary action.

For this reason I thank God for all that is happening through Evangelism-in-Depth. It was my privilege to take part in the Billy Graham Crusades throughout the Caribbean and Central America, at which time Ken Strachan and his colleagues began to look for a new approach to evangelism in Latin America. We on the Billy Graham Team have increasingly been concerned with the way that we can mobilize the church and penetrate society.

The basic concept of Evangelism-in-Depth is not new. I recall a conversation in which I mentioned its thesis, that the growth of any movement is in direct proportion to its ability to mobilize its entire membership for continuous evangelism. A minister seated on one side of me said that he thought he had heard that someplace before. Another minister on the other side chuckled and said that perhaps he had been reading his New Testament!

As I understand it, Evangelism-in-Depth is not mainly a program or a technique, nor is it a trademark with some magical power. Rather, it is a mood, a spirit, a deep conviction born of the Holy Spirit in the hearts of men—men who are ruthlessly honest, who realize the failures of the church to keep up with the galloping birthrate of the world, but who are also realistic enough to know that if we take God at His word and are willing to reevaluate our methods in the light of the New Testament and the demands of the new day, we can confront our generation with the living Christ.

May God use this book, in which my good friend

Dayton Roberts has so vividly given us the story of Evangelism-in-Depth, to share this vision with Christians around the world. The hour is late. May God awaken us.

LEIGHTON FORD

PREFACE

HE HAD AGREED to meet me at O'Hare Airport in Chicago. So I was pleased but not surprised to find Ken Taylor waiting for me as I disembarked and hurried through the crowded terminal. After greeting each other, we ducked into the coffee shop and found a table near the plate glass windows overlooking the apron.

"Well, have you thought about my proposition?" I asked, as soon as we had placed our order. "You've been keenly interested in Evangelism-in-Depth from the very beginning. You encouraged Ken Strachan and Liz Isáis to write a book about the early experiments.* You are a writer, editor—"

"Yes, I know," Ken interrupted me. "Ever since you called me yesterday I have been thinking and praying about it. But I've got at least five more years—or I think I have—of work mapped out ahead of me. As I have prayed, the Lord has given me guidance, not for myself but for you!"

"Now wait a minute!" I said. "I'm glad you're smiling, because you can't be serious. Why, I—"

"But I am serious," Ken went on. "The story of

* *Evangelism in Depth* (Chicago: Moody Press, 1961).

8

Evangelism-in-Depth needs to be told by someone on the inside, who knows it and can interpret it, who speaks Spanish and has access to the files and the people involved."

"Well," I admitted, "we have given some thought to asking someone closer to the action to try to describe it, but we would rather have your objectivity and outside perspective. Besides, you know my schedule. Partly because of your own strong urging I have agreed to travel to Asia with Rubén Lores, and there just isn't the two- or three-month hole in my schedule that I would need to get away and write."

Ken's insistence was not easily parried. "But you don't need two or three months. Do it the way I wrote *Living Letters*."

I was intrigued. "How did you write *Living Letters?*"

"In fifteen-minute snatches on the Northwestern, commuting to and from Chicago. After a while I got into the routine, so that I could turn my mind off and on at will. In the evening I found I could pick up immediately where I had left off in the morning. You could do this job the same way."

"That's all right for you," I countered. "But my mind isn't disciplined like yours—it doesn't work that way!"

"But you could try, couldn't you?" His voice got almost conspiratorial as he went on. "Look, you've got more than a three-hour flight ahead of you to Los Angeles this afternoon. Promise me that you'll take just an hour of that time to write down what you think this book should include and what its purpose should be. And then during the next few days—just on a trial basis—dedicate ten or fifteen minutes a day to writing."

I agreed, and this little book is the result. It is a patchwork of sections dictated in hotel rooms, pounded out at odd moments, and elaborated often at the expense of other responsibilities. Portions have appeared in different form elsewhere. I am indebted to the *Latin America Evangelist* (Latin America Mission) and *The Andean Outlook* (Andes Evangelical Mission) for allowing me to incorporate material from my articles published by them. I am also grateful to the Rev. Marvin Mardock, professor at Azusa Pacific College, Azusa, California, for permission to include excerpts from a chapter prepared for future publication under his editorship.

In these pages the reader will not find a strictly chronological account of the development of Evangelism-in-Depth. I have chosen to start with the death of my beloved brother-in-law, Kenneth Strachan, the human architect of Evangelism-in-Depth, and then to revert by flashback to the early history of the movement.

The story proceeds in order through the first three national Evangelism-in-Depth experiments: Nicaragua (1960), Costa Rica (1961), and Guatemala (1962). Then the chapters become more topical than chronological, although there are historical references, covering: overseas expansion of in-depth evangelism, criticism of the movement, its basic theological principles, and finally, its program. The last chapter is based upon the Bolivian effort (1965).

To keep the record straight, we list the chronology of the Latin American nationwide movements of Evangelism-in-Depth as follows:

1960—Nicaragua
1961—Costa Rica
1962—Guatemala
1963-64—Honduras
1964—Venezuela
1965—Bolivia
1965-66—Dominican Republic
1967—Nicaragua, Atlantic Coast
1967—Peru

I believe the story of these national experiments has something to say to the rest of the Christian world.

It has something to say to the theological pessimists who see us as living in a "post-Christian" era; who think that the day of missionary outreach is past; and who claim that if God is to accomplish His purposes, He must do it through the secularization of the gospel and by His activity in the world rather than through the church.

It has something to say to the liberal "missiologists" who invert the New Testament by their current emphases on the revolutionizing of social structures rather than on the regeneration of individuals.

It has something to say to the "separationism" that builds Christian ghettos, that talks evangelism but "has lost its winsome appeal and has built into it a self-defeating pattern of schism and isolation that aborts the evangelistic invitation by the grimly exclusive attitude with which it is extended."*

Above all, it has something to offer the Christian church wherever it stands confused, without strategy, uncertain as to its mission and how to accomplish it.

*Samuel H. Moffett, "Self-Containment" (paper delivered at World Congress on Evangelism, Berlin, 1966).

Evangelism-in-Depth has been described as the most hopeful contemporary pattern of evangelism, reflecting —despite all the ripples and wrinkles of its human surface—the apostolic vigor of the book of the Acts.

It is high time that evangelism moved to center-stage in our thinking. The essence of the gospel message is its demand for a personal response. God's miracle of redemptive regeneration occurs only when a man voluntarily exposes his cancerous soul to the probing and healing finger of the Saviour. And to challenge all men to do this is the task of evangelistic witness to which the entire body of Christ is called. Together, as Christians, we must find ways and strategies for making that witness more effective.

Because I am convinced of these things, I was easily persuaded to recount the story of what God has done in Latin America through Evangelism-in-Depth. It is a highly personalized story, and no one else—not even the Latin America Mission—should be held responsible for this particular interpretation. I am only one blind man, and the elephant is large!

But it has been a stimulating task. I am grateful to Ken Taylor for getting me started, to my fellow executives, colleagues, and patient secretaries in the LAM for their encouragement and assistance, and to my wife for helping me stick to the job.

The great day foretold by the Prophet Joel and anticipated at Pentecost may well be near. The Spirit of God is moving upon His people. It is time for Christ's church—the whole church to respond, each Christian rising to the challenge.

"Let the weak say, 'I am a warrior'!" (Joel 3:10 RSV).

1

HE LEFT A TEAM

LITERALLY THOUSANDS were gathered for the funeral.

The crowd overflowed the inner sanctuary of the Templo Bíblico, spilling out through the vestibule onto the sidewalks and blocking traffic on the two streets which converged outside the building. The people pressed tightly against each other—tense, solemn, straining to hear what was going on inside. Among them were government officials, educators, artisans, peons, professional men, a Catholic priest, a sister of the president—representatives from every stratum of society.

The hush was natural, spontaneous. They were gathered to pay homage to Kenneth Strachan, their esteemed friend. He had died in California within a year of leaving San José, Costa Rica, where his body had been returned for burial. Memories of his presence were fresh, and the pain of parting acute. Some were asking inwardly why he had been cut off in the prime of life. Others merely resigned themselves to grief or found comfort through their faith in a sovereign and merciful God. They waited, subdued, for the conclusion of the service.

13

Inside the church on the platform, behind the simple gray casket, sat two of the general directors of the Latin America Mission which Strachan had headed, and with them the leaders of its Division of Evangelism. These were the men who had pioneered the Evangelism-in-Depth experiments throughout the continent.

To different ones of that great throng who mourned his passing, Kenneth Strachan had been husband, father, brother, friend and mission executive. In a particular sense, however, to those who sat on the platform he was not only brother and friend; he was their beloved leader, the architect of a hopeful new program of evangelistic outreach. His life and ministry were significant, they realized, not only for them but for Christian missions around the world.

From my place down in front with the family, I watched them with respect and affection. Ken had loved these men—it was his blend of genius and loyalty, plus their devotion to Christ, that bound us together. Horace "Dit" Fenton, himself recently released from the hospital following surgery, was now our spiritual mentor. A peerless expositor of the Word, Dit was also a sharp organization man, full of humor and personal diplomacy. Beside him, Dave Howard— young, energetic, incisive—represented the vigor of the Latin America Mission's leadership. My heart went out to these men in waves of love and sympathy, because I knew what they were thinking and suffering. We were in this together. We had been Ken's closest associates.

But the Latin Americans on the platform were the ones who particularly drew my thoughts. What a team Ken Strachan had recruited and trained! I was proud

14

and grateful to see Rodolfo Cruz, stolid, gray-topped veteran, standing to lead in prayer. Seldom have I met a man more patient, more incorruptible, more faithful in the ministry of Christ—a man whose normal severity had been transformed into ebullience and enthusiasm since five years ago he joined the team to give himself full time to the work of evangelism.

Rubén Lores, his always pale face looking whiter than usual beneath the jet black hair, was the newest member of the team. Now the director of the Latin America Mission's Division of Evangelism, Cuban-born Lores brought to the task a razor-sharp mind, a fertile imagination, and a deep devotional life that both rebuked and encouraged me. I had watched him weep with Ken not many weeks before, and I wept with him today.

Sitting beside him, almost hidden from me behind the pulpit, was Juan Isáis, his unquenchable optimism struggling this afternoon with the grief he felt at Ken's passing. The companion and prayer mate of many a campaign, Juan was closer than a brother. It was Ken who had sensed the young Mexican's potential for leadership and had taught him to mobilize people. They had shared the triumphs and disappointments of nearly fifteen years of evangelism. Together they had seen God work and had learned to trust Him. It was easy to find a warm bond of fellowship with Juan.

Tears rolled unashamed down the rugged face of Jonás González, at the end of the row. My own eyes dimmed also as I remembered some of the Lord's dealings with Jonás as a young man intent on pleasure and a selfish career. Almost as roughly as He reversed the path of the Prophet Jonah in the Old Testament, God

15

had jolted Jonás into the Christian ministry, and two years earlier, after a decade of fruitful experience in a Baptist pastorate in Texas, Jonás had joined Ken Strachan and the Evangelism-in-Depth team.

So different, so complementary, so outstanding— these four men symbolized for me the emerging Christian leadership of the fast-growing evangelical church in Latin America. As far as can be determined, at the beginning of the nineteenth century there were no Protestant Christians in Spanish and Portuguese America. Now there were perhaps fifteen million. God had been at work in marvelous ways.

In a peculiar sense the life of Ken Strachan had been linked to this unusual growth of the Latin American evangelical church. He was born in 1910, the year of the famous Edinburgh Missionary Conference from whose agenda Latin America was excluded as not being a legitimate mission field. Indeed, it remained for some time the forgotten continent of Protestant missions.

Although the 1910 error was later officially rectified, even by 1936 when Ken Strachan came to the mission field the evangelical population of Latin America was less than 2,500,000. By then, however, the foundations for growth had been laid, and after World War II the Christian community surged ahead in an ever-increasing torrent, until by 1965 there were an estimated fifteen million evangelical Christians—this in a continent which for four hundred years had been an absolute and impregnable fortress of Roman Catholic superstition and folk religion.

Of this phenomenal growth, Kenneth Strachan was both observer and participant. A missionary colleague, historian Dr. Wilton M. Nelson, cites one of the significant factors extending the rapid expansion of Protestantism during this period: "The rise of a more aggressive evangelism which the fiery and fearless Scotchman, Harry Strachan (founder of the Latin America Mission), pioneered in the dramatic campaigns which he organized and directed, especially during the years 1920 to 1934." This was the atmosphere in which Kenneth's childhood was nourished.

"Previous to this time," Dr. Nelson continues, "it seemed that evangelical missions in Latin America had become institutionalized or had reached an impasse, and were suffering from an inferiority complex due to the strong popular prejudice and opposition they had suffered."†

Kenneth's revival, after his father's death, of the program of evangelistic campaigns under the sponsorship of the Latin America Mission, was one more contributing factor to the further growth of the Protestant movement. But it was for the larger concept of Evangelism-in-Depth that he would be remembered not only by his Latin American colleagues but by fellow missionaries around the world.

It would have been natural for any observer at this impressive funeral service to make a mental comparison of Ken Strachan with the father whom he had now joined in the presence of the Lord. For almost thirty years he had labored as a missionary under the shadow of his famous father.

A talented and untiring evangelist, Harry Strachan, as ubiquitous as the fabled don Quixote, had moved

† "Evangelical Surge in Latin America," *Christianity Today*, VII, No. 21, July 19, 1963, p. 5 [1009].

up and down the continent in unceasing evangelistic activity, setting up, coordinating, and carrying on evangelistic campaigns in all the principal cities of Latin America. He was advance man, follow-up man, coordinator, master of ceremonies, song leader, promoter, and sometimes the evangelist himself, although generally he used outstanding Latin American preachers as evangelists in his campaigns.

Harry Strachan was a hard-driving Scotchman, with a tenacity and courage equal to every circumstance. By dint of hard work and midnight study, he conquered the Spanish language as few foreigners have done.

When he discovered that his rather severe Scotch nature was a handicap in evangelistic work, he sought from the Lord and received a gift of spiritual empathy which endeared him to his Latin as well as his Anglo-Saxon colleagues. A remarkable man of commanding presence and irresistible authority, Harry Strachan's ministry in the Spanish-speaking countries of Latin America will never be forgotten.

This was the man under whose shadow Kenneth labored. For him it was not an easy road. So small of stature that in college he acquired the nickname "Squirt," Kenneth lacked his father's commanding pulpit presence, his singing voice, his natural authority, and his ability as a preacher and evangelist. Little wonder that he should be plagued all his life by an inferiority complex in this area of his ministry.

Nevertheless, to the observer at his funeral it must have been apparent that God had caused Kenneth's incapabilities to become his greatest asset. Whereas Father Strachan was unable to recruit permanent help

18

in evangelism—although evangelical leadership was admittedly scarce in his day—Kenneth had left an outstanding team seated behind his coffin on the platform.

Father Strachan had shared the vision with many of his contemporaries, but he was unable to find those to whom he could pass on his particular burden of responsibility for the evangelization of the whole of Latin America. In a very real sense he stood alone in the task. With the declining health of his latter years the evangelistic efforts of the Latin America Mission waned, and it was not until five years after his death that the Holy Spirit burdened Kenneth to take up his father's battle.

Son Kenneth, on the other hand, had not only caught the vision and implemented it but had communicated it to his colleagues. As a result he left an organized, experienced and competent Division of Evangelism to carry on the task which God had committed to his hands.

The funeral sermon was preached by Rubén Lores. He used as the basis of his meditation the story of the fiery chariot which had taken Elijah from earth to the presence of God. This he likened to the cruel suffering and anguish of Kenneth's final illness. But in one place the analogy stopped.

"Elijah," Lores said, "passed on his mantle to a single prophet, Elisha, but Kenneth Strachan has passed his mantle to a host of colleagues today engaged with him in the all-out evangelistic task."

Increasing mention around the world of Evangelism-in-Depth confirmed the truth of Lores' observation. From nearly thirty countries outside of Latin America had come correspondence requesting information, sharing insights, asking questions about Evangelism-in-Depth.

In Africa's Nigeria the "New Life for All" movement was reaping unprecedented blessings from God and a harvest of souls.

A city-to-city crusade of evangelism in Belgium was seeking to apply in-depth methods in that country.

In the state of Maharashtra in India another Evangelism-in-Depth experiment was under way, and still another in Korea.

From Portugal, Lebanon, Taiwan, Japan, the Philippines, Appalachia and Great Britain came testimony that Ken Strachan's mantle had indeed fallen not on one or two, nor yet a half dozen successors, but upon a host of colleagues who had received from God through his vision and ministry new insights into the evangelistic task, a new burden to press onto the fulfillment of the Great Commission, and a new understanding of how this might be done.

Ken himself would have been surprised at Lores' observation. He was slow to recognize his successes and quick to judge his failures. Instead of dwelling on Evangelism-in-Depth's apparent popularity, his mind probably would have gone back to what he considered the biggest failure of all—the 1952 campaign in Nicaragua, where his father had previously won his first successes in international evangelism, and where later Evangelism-in-Depth was to become a successful reality.

To Kenneth, for a long time, Nicaragua had spelled frustration and failure.

2

FRUSTRATION, FAILURE

THE DC-3 growled down the runway and lifted off into the west. From his seat just behind the wing, Ken Strachan watched the familiar Costa Rican landmarks recede into the distance—first the dark green coffee acreage adjoining the Sabana airport; then the narrow-gauge railroad, the Virilla River, the town of Heredia, and finally the city of Alajuela, as the plane attained its altitude and veered slightly to the north on its course to Nicaragua.

But Ken was not paying too much attention to the lovely plateau beneath him. His mind was already in Nicaragua, grappling with the problems that awaited his arrival. It was 1952 and the city-wide evangelistic campaign in Managua, currently being sponsored by the Latin America Mission, was off to a bad start. Managua, Nicaragua's capital, was not a large city, and it had seemed that this would be an easy campaign to set up, but from the beginning everything had gone wrong.

In the first place, the evangelist he had engaged had proved unacceptable to the Nicaraguan committee. There had been denominational tensions, and some

21

had disliked the preacher's style. Admittedly he had not put his best foot forward in Managua, and the dissatisfaction of the Nicaraguans was to a degree understandable.

So the evangelist moved on to Honduras, and for several nights it was necessary to fill in the Managua schedule with substitute preachers, a young Mexican on the Latin America Mission staff carrying most of the load. From neighboring Costa Rica, evangelist Israel García was rushed into the breach.

Ken had been sure that with this substitution things would get back on their feet, and he was encouraged to feel that the Nicaraguan problems were settled. Then disaster struck again. García preached one evening, but after the service he had an attack of appendicitis and was rushed to the hospital for surgery.

Once again, the campaign was carried on by substitutes. Several different preachers were called into action, and now it seemed necessary for Strachan himself to see what he could do to salvage the rather unfortunate situation.

As he watched the volcanic peaks of Nicaragua slide slowly past his airplane window, Ken asked himself, as he had many times before, how he had ever gotten involved in this type of ministry. This was definitely not his dish, and as general director of the mission he had plenty of other responsibilities. Yet he would never be able to shake the conviction borne in upon him by the Holy Spirit that somehow this mass evangelistic ministry must be carried on.

He remembered how God had led his father to leave a successful pastoral ministry in Argentina in order to spark a continent-wide movement of cooperative evangelism. These efforts had been singularly blessed by God in fruitfulness. Then the war had clamped down on transportation, and with the failing health of Father Strachan, the Latin American Evangelization Campaign, now known as the Latin America Mission, had concentrated its efforts along other significant lines— a seminary, radio and literature, and numberless other local activities.

Ken tried to tell himself that these were just as important for God's work as the evangelistic campaigns; yet again and again, in ways completely beyond his expectation, the Holy Spirit had hammered home the responsibility for reviving and maintaining a continental evangelistic outreach.

Ken had been outwardly obedient, but inwardly he often rebelled at the task God seemed to be thrusting upon him. In fact, the summons from Nicaragua caught him in a period of spiritual depression. Scarcely a year before, following the death of his mother, he had been named general director of the Latin America Mission. He had honestly resisted the appointment, feeling himself incapable, but he could get no one to agree with him. The weight of responsibility now was heavy on his shoulders, and torn by inner conflicts, his health had broken. When the cabled SOS from Managua reached him he was vacationing under doctor's orders, not greatly comforted by the realization that his physical symptoms were probably of psychosomatic origin. Certainly he was not in the slightest degree anxious to become personally involved in the Nicaragua campaign.

So here is Ken Strachan, he thought, as the plane carried him closer to the firing line, *small of stature, reticent of personality, headed for Nicaragua to pinch-hit as an evangelist! Why can't I spend my life teaching, writing, or doing research in a library?*

For me to be in this slot, he thought to himself, *is like asking a jockey to play fullback on the Notre Dame football team. Can this really be God's will for me?*

The sense of rebellion had not been totally quelled when his plane touched down and he was met at the Managua airport by Gordon Houser, the faithful but frustrated coordinator of the Managua campaign. As they rode back to the city in a taxi, Houser filled him in on the details of the local situation. Evangelist García was out of danger but was also out of circulation, hospitalized for several more days. The local sponsoring committee was torn by dissension and dissatisfaction, and the results of the campaign thus far had been disappointing.

True, the children's rallies had been highly successful. And, strangely enough, attendance at the meetings had held up amazingly well. The advertising had been good and the public impact considerable. The whole city was aware that an evangelistic campaign was in full swing, and with two more nights to go it looked as though God could yet bring victory in this very difficult situation. For that night, arrangements had already been made, and someone else had been drafted to preach the evangelistic message, but for the next night, the closing meeting, they were counting on Strachan to be the evangelist.

Ken only had time for a bit of rest, to freshen up at the hotel, and to visit Israel García in his hospital room before he was driven to the athletic field of the Baptist high school, where the campaign meetings were being held. The place was centrally located in the city and had been nicely arranged with ample space for the thousands of curiosity seekers and others who would drop in to hear what the Protestant evangelist was saying. Lights had been carefully rigged and the platform located in order to insure maximum audibility for the congregation.

Strachan was pleased with all of this, but as he unobtrusively left the platform following the opening of the evening service and made his way to the edge of the crowd, he was conscious that things were far from right. There was no obvious evidence of the Holy Spirit's presence. The impromptu evangelist seemed to be struggling with his message, and the people, while attentive, were not responsive.

From his vantage point at the rear of the open-air sanctuary, Strachan reflected on the frailties and the problems of such evangelistic efforts. So much seemed to depend not on the visiting team but on the local committee, on the preparations and the follow-up, on the amount of enthusiasm and dedication which were brought locally to the task, on the degree of involvement of pastors and churches in the crusade. Somehow it seemed almost futile even to pray for great victory if the local situation were not adequately prepared to receive the Lord's blessing.

At the end of the service, despite a prolonged invitation a scant half dozen people found their way to the platform for consultation with the evangelist. With a heavy heart, Strachan returned to his hotel room to pray about his responsibility for the coming evening and to seek God's will for his own ministry and that of the crusade. The late hours of prayer and Bible study, however, together with more of the same the following morning, brought Strachan a new confidence that God would yet answer prayer and bring great fruitfulness to this ministry in Managua.

As he struggled in intercession, he came to the conviction that God would be pleased to have him claim specifically the salvation of fifty souls at the closing evangelistic meeting of the campaign. So there was a spring in his step as he made his way back to the hospital in the afternoon to visit Israel García.

"Israel," he said, as he walked into the latter's room in the hospital, "I believe God is going to bless us in an unusual way tonight."

Israel's face lit up, and with an enthusiastic smile he replied, "Don Kenneth, God has led me to believe the same thing and to claim specifically the salvation of fifty people. All day, I have been thanking God that fifty souls are going to respond at tonight's meeting."

This seemed to be a remarkable confirmation of his own convictions and it was with high spirits and expectations that Ken made his way to the meeting place and took his seat on the platform when the time for the evening service came. The threat of rain was in the air, but God had promised a great victory that night. Besides, the rainy season had not yet begun. God could be trusted to provide good weather for this tremendous evangelistic opportunity.

Soon the music, singing and announcements were finished. As Strachan came to the pulpit to preach, he sensed a new freedom and a new responsiveness on the part of the crowd. He preached as he had seldom preached before, and worked up confidently toward the climax when he would be giving the invitation.

So engrossed had he become in his message, however, that he did not at first notice the dark clouds building up to one side. Soon the rumble of thunder became ominous and, sensing the restlessness of his audience, he called out, "I know it looks like rain, but don't move. God won't let it rain until He has won a victory here tonight. Stay right where you are. Rain or no rain, I'm going to stay right here to do business for God. Now how many—"

Scarcely were the words out of his mouth when a tremendous tropical shower burst on the crowd. Instantly—almost before he knew what had happened— the great audience disappeared, seeking shelter under the eaves of the nearest buildings.

The preacher too was forced to run to escape drenching under the sudden downpour. As he huddled, damp and miserable, under the eaves of the adjoining classroom building, Strachan was left with all his doubts and questions about the present and future of mass evangelism and of God's peculiar dealings with those engaged in this type of ministry.

He felt personally disillusioned. Even more deeply he felt that Managua, indeed all of Nicaragua, had been defrauded in this particular campaign by a series of circumstances which could have been either diabolical or the result of improper planning on the part of his mission.

Did things really have to be this way? Was this God's plan for evangelism? Was there no better method? Was this what God had called him to? And the mission? Was God really on his side? Did He truly answer prayer? Were His promises and assurances mere mockery?

It was a chastened Ken Strachan who for the next few years headed the ambitious evangelistic thrust of the Latin America Mission.

3

REFLECTION, HOPE

THE YEAR 1959 was a year of reflection. The Latin America Mission's Division of Evangelism and particularly its leader, Kenneth Strachan, had been too busy to back off and reevaluate their evangelistic strategy. The preceding decade had been packed full of almost continuous intensive evangelistic effort in many of the largest cities of Latin America.

Outstanding evangelists, musicians, chalk artists, promoters and administrators had combined to leave the challenge of the gospel of Christ echoing in the hearts of multitudes throughout the continent. Phil Saint had sketched the gospel in vivid chalk colors under the Barbadian stars. Anton Marco had donned his operatic costume and lifted the "Toreador Song" into the highest tiers of the Ciudad Juarez bullring and then had galvanized his Mexican audience with a moving rendition of "I'd Rather Have Jesus."

In the concert halls and national theaters of places like Lima and Viña del Mar, Richard Foulkes had interpreted Chopin and Debussy with a depth and dexterity that underlined with convincing authority his testimony to the grace of Jesus Christ. Evangelists like

Israel García, Eliseo Hernández and Juan Isáis gave eloquent witness to the power of the gospel.

Buenos Aires, Rosario, Tandil, Santiago, Caracas, Guayaquil, Guatemala and many other cities had heard, as never before, the claims of Christ pressed upon them. Bullrings, theaters, churches and open-air plazas had been used to give out the good news to thousands upon thousands who would not otherwise have heard. Sacred and classical concerts, religious and evangelistic films—these as well as the more conventional methods of evangelistic preaching were used to give as wide an outreach to the gospel as possible.

Strachan's favorite Scripture verse during these years was, "He who sows sparingly shall also reap sparingly; and he who sows bountifully shall also reap bountifully" (II Cor. 9:6 NAS). It was therefore with unbounded enthusiasm, lavish promotion, but careful evangelistic techniques withal, as well as with humble and sincere dependence upon God and the ministry of the Holy Spirit, that the evangelistic efforts of the Latin America Mission were carried on during the decade of the 1950's, with a normal measure of blessing and disappointment.

The climax of this era came in the early months of 1958, when under Strachan's leadership the Latin America Mission spearheaded and coordinated the Billy Graham Caribbean Crusade. This was a fabulous operation, something like an international evangelistic fugue, as advance workers moved from island to island and country to country, followed by evangelists from the Billy Graham team, who conducted full-scale evangelistic campaigns. Each was climaxed, in turn, by a two- or three-day visit by Billy Graham himself.

Who could forget the surging excitement of those days? The challenge of getting Christians to think big, plan big and pray big. The warm fellowship that grew across denominational lines. The pressure of dates and deadlines. The timeless wonder and worship of all-night prayer meetings. The excitement of radio and television programs. The thousand and one details. Most of all, the deep awareness that the Holy Spirit was at work through it all, fashioning men and circumstances to His purpose.

Thus the campaigns began with Leighton Ford in Jamaica, Grady Wilson in Barbados, and Joe Blinco in Trinidad, conducting almost simultaneous two-week crusades. At the same time, in Spanish-speaking Puerto Rico, Israel García was the speaker at the opening meetings of a campaign there. Billy Graham then went to Jamaica to wind up the highly successful meetings on that island, as Leighton Ford moved to Panama to start a new crusade on the isthmus. Subsequently the teams moved on successively to Costa Rica and Guatemala, and then concluded in Mexico.

For many years Strachan had been interested in Billy Graham's campaign efforts in other parts of the world, and he had finally made a special trip to the States to observe a campaign personally and to talk with Dr. Graham. A strong friendship grew out of those early associations, and the Latin America Mission personnel gained much from the careful and Spirit-led methodology of the Graham team. It was a tremendous learning experience, and God's blessing was very evident throughout the tour.

Following this period of extremely intensive evangelistic activity during the first part of 1958, it had been decided to schedule no further campaigns for the rest of 1958 nor for 1959. Rather, a year was to be given to prayer and reflection on the evangelistic ministry of the mission and to taking stock of past victories and failures. Strachan was not satisfied. There remained an elusive dimension of thought just beyond his reach. Even the results of the Billy Graham tour had been spotty—far more successful in some countries than in others, the impact more permanent in some areas than in others.

He felt compelled to call a temporary halt in activities and to think creatively about evangelistic strategy. An effort had to be made to evolve a program of evangelistic outreach, he reasoned, that would be more consistent in its positive fruits and more adequate to meet the challenge of a fast-growing population and the rising social revolution in Latin America.

During these months of recess, several of the members of the Division of Evangelism took furloughs, and Strachan dedicated himself to research on the life of his parents and the early years of the mission. It was his intention to write a history of the senior Strachans and of the mission's beginnings. He took advantage of this time also to travel to a number of places where unusual growth had been seen in the Protestant church. With a Costa Rican pastor he journeyed to El Salvador and for a time observed at first hand the outstanding work of the Assemblies of God—their system of church planting, of evangelism, of literature colportage, and the way in which the Holy Spirit had blessed their ministry with remarkable and spontaneous growth.

He had previously journeyed to Chile where he had

been able to study the work of the *Canutos*—the Pentecostal brethren who are famous for their street meetings, for their zeal in personal witness, and for a prodigious church growth. In about 1909, Ken had learned, a Methodist missionary experienced some unusual manifestations of the Holy Spirit and with a small group of followers was forced to withdraw from the Methodist church in Chile. Now, while the original Methodist church had a membership of roughly eight thousand people, the church formed by the missionary and subsequently nourished entirely from indigenous sources estimated its membership at approximately 700,000. Strachan was intrigued by these experiences as he studied how churches could be challenged and motivated to take advantage of the evangelistic opportunities on every hand.

He also became increasingly alarmed over the fast spread of the cults in Latin America—Jehovah's Witnesses, for example, and the Mormons—and he tried to discern what gave them such remarkable growth.

Gradually as he observed these and other groups expanding rapidly in the Latin-American context, and as he studied the archives concerning his own father's evangelistic ministry, Strachan came to realize that the concept of abundant sowing and abundant reaping had to be applied not only to the ministry of the professional evangelist but also, somehow, to the individual Christian as well. Slowly his thinking shifted from "breadth" to "depth" in evangelism.

Through the preceding years every effort had been made to broaden, to enhance, to strengthen the impact of the professional evangelist in a given city or area. New skills of promotion and communication; wiser use of literature, radio and television; better techniques of handling crowds, physical arrangements, public-address systems, follow-up and counseling procedures—all had been developed in an effort to add the greater dimension of breadth to the ministry of Spirit-filled evangelists.

But with this, Strachan was not satisfied. The task was not being accomplished fast enough. The job was not being done. He came to see that a basic principle of growth was being overlooked, and as he studied the fast-growing churches, sects and ideologies, it became apparent that a common underlying principle was observable. He stated it this way: "The growth of any movement is in direct proportion to the success of that movement in mobilizing its total membership in the constant propagation of its beliefs."

It became clearer to Ken as he meditated on these things that it would be necessary to shift the spotlight from the pulpit to the pew in the evangelistic task, from the preacher to the believer, from the evangelist to the ordinary Christian, in an effort to mobilize him in evangelistic outreach, and thus to give a new dimension of depth to the evangelistic effort.

These ideas at first were not easily understood nor articulated. They were born gradually out of the internal struggle in Strachan's soul as he sought objectively to examine his own ministry and that of the mission. It would not be fair to assume that at this point of reassessment he would willingly have been persuaded that mass evangelism was not worth the effort. This was not true. He had too often seen God's hand of blessing in marvelous ways upon the campaigns of the mission and of other groups. Nevertheless, God certainly must have something better, something less spotty, less sporadic, more certain, more church-centered and more permanent than what had often been his and the mission's experience.

In this struggle, as he dug into the Scriptures and labored over the correspondence of his father and the records relating to the early evangelistic campaigns, God gave him the gift of faith to understand the significance of three simple truths. He had probably always "believed" them in a theoretical sense. But now his experience had conditioned him to accept them as basic and dynamic principles of evangelistic activity. They were: first, that Christians *can* work together; second, that when they do, even a tiny minority can make an impact on an entire nation; and third, that this job must be directed largely by local leaders, whose potential in most cases was yet to be appreciated.

He had found that, despite the many problems and difficulties involved, it had indeed been possible to unite almost the total evangelical community of the Caribbean area to back the Billy Graham evangelistic effort. This being the case, it was not hard to believe that it could be done for another campaign and in other areas as well.

At the same time there began to grow in his mind the certainty that even in countries where the evangelicals are a tiny minority, somehow by God's grace if they can work together they can make an impact on the entire nation. The original commission of Christ to His apostles was in terms of the nations of the world. He said, "Go therefore and disciple all nations" (Matt. 28:19, marginal).

This "national" vision, so strong in the ministry of pioneers like William Carey and Hudson Taylor, seemed to be missing from the fractionalized missionary efforts of today, with their local concerns and their comity agreements. Strachan's own imagination began to get excited as he dreamed of believers uniting so firmly in their evangelistic resolve that in truth they could shake a nation as the apostles had shaken the world after Pentecost.

A rereading of Roland Allen's classics on missionary strategy had confirmed a conviction born in his own experience that Latin Americans can best be mobilized by Latin Americans. Foreign missionaries were often too negative in their attitude. This stifled initiative, enthusiasm and creativity on the part of national leaders. Far too frequently their own culture and perspective made missionaries blind to latent leadership potential in persons of other cultural contexts. Their own standards, yardsticks, background and experience— valuable in so many ways—seemed to serve as blinders when it came to spotting Latin American leadership potential.

His studies and reflections were interrupted by the welcome visit of close friends from the United States, Charles and Corabel Morgan, with their two boys. Taking advantage of the occasion, the men and older boys of the two families set off by car on a vacation trip to Nicaragua.

For Strachan, however, it was not all play. Thoughts concerning evangelism were churning in his mind and heart. It occurred to him as they drove across the western cattle country of Costa Rica toward the Nicaraguan border that while the twelve Israelite spies had no Chevrolet station wagon to facilitate their travel, theirs had been a very similar mission.

Strachan and Charles Morgan were going to Nicaragua to spy out the land for God, and to attempt to find an answer to these questions: Can evangelism be deep as well as broad in its impact? Is there a way of mobilizing the total evangelical community in witness? Is it possible to really shake an entire nation for Jesus Christ? Can the impact of the gospel on a nation be measured in total terms? Can this be done by the national leaders? Can a movement be begun that will insure a continuing witness for Jesus Christ across the land?

The exploratory trip was encouraging. Problems began to dissipate. The objectives began to look attainable. By March of 1959, some time before any official commitment was to be given, Strachan knew in his heart that Nicaragua was the promised land of in-depth experiment.

God would yet answer His servant's prayer of faith for a disillusioned evangelist, a "defrauded" city, and a still needy nation.

4

FIRST EXPERIMENT

Now IT WAS a Monday afternoon in March, 1960.

Hot winds were throwing up clouds of dust in the plaza of the little Nicaraguan town of Rivas. That night evangelistic crusades were getting under way in six different cities of the republic. In spite of their small numbers, the Christian forces in Rivas, sparked by the fine leadership of some Nazarene missionaries, had courageously decided to launch their campaign with a parade through the main streets of the city— no light undertaking in Roman Catholic Latin America.

"When we arrived that afternoon at the scheduled point of departure," Strachan recalled, "there were only a few clusters of believers looking rather scared and subdued. Even I was feeling butterflies in my stomach. But, little by little, groups from surrounding villages began coming in, carrying Nicaraguan flags, texts, slogans and their church banners.

"After a short wait we started off, headed by a few cars, a small band on foot, some young flag bearers on horseback, and followed by hundreds of believers marching on foot with their flags and banners. We sang as we marched past Central Park and the Cathe-

dral, by the army barracks, along the main streets of
the city. Soldiers, police and citizens lined the sidewalks and looked on with amazement. The band in
front was doing its best with 'Onward, Christian Soldiers.' And those near us were singing out the words
in Spanish, 'With the cross of Jesus going on before.'"

Farther down the line they were singing the theme
chorus that had swept the country, "Nicaragua será
para Cristo" ("Nicaragua shall belong to Christ"). A
block or so behind, others were singing also; all were
singing, and it made an impressive sound never before
heard in the streets of that city.

"I felt a thrill of pride," Strachan added, "to be walk-
ing beside those Nicaraguan Christians in their brave
and dignified witness for Christ."

That night a great crowd was present in the plaza
for the opening meeting of the campaign. With joy
the gospel hymns rang out under the leadership of
Vern Van Hovel from radio station HCJB in Quito,
Ecuador. Christians were thrilled to hear the simple,
powerful preaching of Rubén Lores, at that time from
New York City, as he held the crowd spellbound with
the clear claims of the gospel. In five other centers
something similar was taking place, with more than a
dozen other outstanding evangelists and gospel singers
who had come from a number of neighboring countries to help out.

As he stood on the edge of the crowd, Strachan's
mind went back over the previous weeks of intensive
preparation which had led up to this moment. He was
particularly grateful for the untiring efforts of Juan
and Elisabeth Isáis. In Juan Isáis, then acting director
of the Latin America Mission's Division of Evangelism,

the Lord had given Strachan the ideal colleague for heading the Nicaraguan experiment. A *simpático* Mexican of boundless energy, he brought to the job a natural optimism and a supernatural faith which were enthusiastically contagious. He combined executive gifts and a sharp sense of organization with a versatility equal to any situation—songleading, soloing, preaching—together with a loyalty to the mission and a personal affection for Strachan that made them a great administrative and evangelistic team. Juan's wife, Elisabeth, rounded out the enterprise with her talent at the piano and her outstanding journalistic capabilities.

As the hush of the evangelistic service continued, Strachan recalled also the enthusiastic cooperation of the Nicaraguan committee and especially of its president, Dr. Rodolfo Mejía, vice-president of the National Bank of Nicaragua and an outstanding Baptist layman. How could he ever thank God sufficiently for the response of Nicaraguan leaders to the challenge of Evangelism-in-Depth? He remembered the tremendous job of training hundreds of them which had been carried out by George Sánchez, Sam Clark and others of The Navigators.

The splendid visitation campaign sparked by John Thomas came to mind. He thanked God silently for Bill Thompson's leadership on the Atlantic Coast, for Dorothy Andrews' help in the central office, and for the contribution made by all the other pastors and missionaries. He felt a sense of deep gratitude to them and to those in the homeland who with their prayers and gifts had made this effort possible.

His mind also went back a generation as he thought of his father, Harry Strachan, who had pioneered campaigns in Rivas thirty-five years before, and he wondered if he might be looking down on the scene that night, rejoicing with the angels in heaven over souls that were being saved.

Altogether it was a happy experience. They were in the midst of an experiment that might result in a new strategy of evangelism for Latin America—a plan of action that would enlist the Latin American Christians themselves, working out of their local church centers, uniting their forces for all-out efforts aimed at fulfilling the Great Commission in their own countries.

They were wondering as they carried out their evangelistic assignments in Nicaragua if this might not offer the key whereby the church of Christ in these tremendous days of revolutionary opportunity might be able to meet the challenge of the exploding populations without Christ and without hope in the world.

Others too were asking the same questions. This first experiment of Evangelism-in-Depth in Nicaragua was observed with penetrating interest from all sides. Christians throughout Latin America watched to see whether or not the plan might be worth trying in their own countries. Mission authorities in the United States, of both denominational and faith missions, followed it cautiously to see if such cooperation on a national scale would help rather than hurt their work. A number of key evangelicals from the United States made it a point to stop by Nicaragua to see for themselves.

What, after all, did happen in Nicaragua to be worth so much attention?

A prominent bacteriologist, son of a Nicaraguan Christian family but until recently not an open believer himself, said, "Nobody could have ignored this effort. Everybody is talking about it everywhere I travel, either for or against, but they have to talk."

A full-time Bible colporteur said, "What was done in five months wouldn't have been accomplished otherwise in ten years, nor even twenty."

A pastor in the capital city: "I believed I had finished my ministry. But now Evangelism-in-Depth has awakened me. I am living again!"

Another pastor: "The impact that Evangelism-in-Depth has made on the whole country is a big thing, the like of which we've never seen before."

A missionary: "I am infinitely grateful to God for the revival it brought to me personally."

In some ways Evangelism-in-Depth in Nicaragua was a complicated effort. In essence, however, it simply attempted to put into practice the peculiar genius of Christianity that makes every believer responsible for the spiritual welfare of his neighbor. It called for total mobilization of the Christian forces of the country.

As Strachan reported on events in Nicaragua he referred to some basic considerations which he had outlined before Evangelism-in-Depth got under way:

> (1) Rather than think in terms of a continent, we ought to think in *specific terms of national or regional territories.* It's always easy to talk in lofty terms of world evangelism, but as soon as we specify a certain territory we face the practical realities and demands of the job. We can no longer talk about evangelism but are forced to count our resources and roll up our sleeves and get to work. Furthermore, it is always easier to tackle the problems of cooperation in a local and national situation than in a world or international

one. [This made **Nicaragua with its** modest population of less than one and a half million an ideal target.]

(2) In each country the key to total evangelization, we concluded, lay not with the foreign missionary organizations or even the national ministers—important as both of these were—but with the sum total of the Christian believers. If the key to world evangelism is a reproductive witness of the totality of the individual believers, then our first objective had to be *to mobilize and train these Christians* for effective continuous witness in their own countries.

(3) This individual witness needed to be carried out both in everyday life and in special endeavor *within the total witness of the local Christian community* [*the local congregation*]. This made it necessary to impart to pastors and church members everywhere the new and more Scripturally correct concept of the mission of the local church. Each local church, made up of a group of Christians led by their officers and pastor, had to be conceived of not as the passive recipients of the ministry of their pastor, but as a unit for a continuous, spontaneous, and planned witnessing and evangelism under his leadership.

(4) Another consideration that weighed greatly upon us was the necessity of bringing together the different church bodies and organizations in a *united witness.*

In Roman Catholic Latin America, where the enemies of the Gospel are continuously pointing out to us our divisions and dissensions and holding them up as proof of the fact that we do not and cannot represent the true church—and where the outward unity and uniformity of the Roman Catholic Church was cited as proof of her Apostolic and Catholic claims—it is all the more essential for evangelical Christians to give some tangible witness of their oneness in Christ.

We realized that the problems of co-operation were not easy ones to solve. . . . doctrinal and other practical differences . . . We did not feel that these could be minimized. . . . we believed, nevertheless, that it was necessary to give some united witness to the Gospel, and it was our conviction that in the field of evangelism, at least, cooperation was not only possible, but essential.

(5) Finally, it was our conviction that the individual activity of all the believers and all the local churches and the co-operative efforts of the sum of the different churches had all to be *related to one over-all plan and strategy* that would aim at nothing less than the total and effective evangelization of the territory selected.[*]

It was with these considerations in mind that the planners had drawn up the tentative five-month program which was now approaching its conclusion.

Evangelism-in-Depth had been publicly launched in Nicaragua with a special week-long conference for Christian workers, missionaries, pastors, lay leaders and their wives. This had been a long time not only of instruction and of inspiration, but also of heart-searching and revival, concluded by an all-night prayer meeting and the Lord's Supper. Hearts had been melted, divisions healed, and the presence of the Holy Spirit manifested in new courage, new zeal, new optimism, new unity and a new disposition to do battle for Jesus Christ.

The theme song of the movement, written by the national coordinator, Juan Isáis, proclaimed a lofty goal: "Nicaragua Shall Belong to Christ!" How impossible it sounded, especially in traditionally Roman Catholic territory! But as the Latin melody filled the

[*] *Evangelism in Depth* (Chicago: Moody Press, 1961), pp. 27-29.

air at the united meetings of Evangelism-in-Depth, and as enthusiastic voices more nearly shouted than sang the words, it suddenly seemed that the power of God might be sufficient to make it come true. Yes, of course, the power of God *was* sufficient—if everyone would do his part.

> We shall win Nicaragua for Jesus
> If united we labor for Him;
> All the nation shall honor the Saviour
> And show forth His great power over sin.
> To the fight, then, with holy devotion,
> Preaching Christ to the lost everywhere!
> Loyal Christians, unite!
> Save our land for the right!
> For the Lord shall soon appear.

The pastors' retreat was quickly followed by a period of mobilization in organizing prayer cells throughout the country. In daily or weekly gatherings of three to eight persons each, the Nicaraguan Christians united in intercession for unsaved friends, relatives and neighbors. Then a training program was set up for the purpose of preparing each believer for personal and visitation evangelism as well as for active participation in the united crusades and follow-up which would come later.

The next stage of the program called for a series of united evangelistic crusades in each of the strategic centers of the country. It was one of these that had brought the believers together in the city of Rivas.

Finally, a campaign was held in the capital city of Managua. Afterward, in the follow-up period, local churches were encouraged to carry out their own evangelistic meetings, renew their visitation work, and continue in the pattern of total purposeful witness and outreach that would result in constant growth and expansion.

By the time Evangelism-in-Depth ended in May, 1960, five months after the official kickoff on New Year's Eve, it would have been an exaggeration to claim that Nicaragua had been won for Christ, or even that the entire Christian church had been mobilized. But thousands of Christians had done battle for their Lord, many for the first time, and what He had accomplished through them was impressive. A Nicaraguan layman wrote:

> There has been wonderful fruit: consecration of lives that were swept into activity they had never carried out before; reconciliation of brethren who had been separated; new spiritual births which took place in the 1,904 conversions recorded in the campaigns. There was also a determined sense of unity among those of us who are members of the family of Christ. We could say much more, but it can all be summed up in a single sentence: The Lord Jesus Christ was manifested in power, and the Holy Spirit worked marvels.

Actually, more than 2,500 people had made decisions to accept Christ through the evangelistic campaigns, personal visits to their homes, or other special meetings related to the impact of Evangelism-in-Depth.

Five hundred prayer groups had come into being in neighborhoods throughout the country, some with such blessing that they were to continue for months.

More than two thousand Christians had sat through a series of eight training classes and had felt their spiritual life quickened and their responsibilities as Christ's ambassadors underlined.

More than 65,000 Nicaraguan homes had been visited and three times that many Scripture portions and tracts given out, plus thousands of handbills advertising the campaigns.

Fourteen united evangelistic crusades had been held —with an aggregate attendance of 126,000—in towns all over the country and in the capital city of Managua. They were campaigns full of "firsts," but they were different in each place. Some examples: the first time all the churches in the area had gotten together for a campaign; the first time a public plaza had been obtained for an evangelical meeting; the first time evangelicals had dared to stage a parade; the first time airplanes had dropped evangelical propaganda; the first time secular radio stations had broadcast evangelical meetings. The greatest "first" of all was that for the first time Nicaraguans became aware of the Christians and the Christians' message in their midst.

What happened in Nicaragua was, in a sense, what every Christian leader would like to see happen in his part of the world. It was a daring plan, carried out, as one pastor put it, "with the defects that human beings always have." But perhaps its strongest point was precisely that; in spite of problems, errors in judgment, lack of personnel, limited funds and all the rest, Evangelism-in-Depth had captured the imagination and stirred the enthusiasm of God's people, with the result that the church surged forward and the message of Christ went out as never before to the inhabitants of a spiritually hungry country in Central America.

There were many lessons yet to be learned. The

road ahead was long and rough, but Strachan and his colleagues knew that in some measure God had given a positive answer to the questions they had raised, and that they had been privileged to witness the very early beginnings of what others would later call the most hopeful and creative approach to the evangelistic task yet to be seen.

5

NOT WITHOUT HONOR

"A prophet is not without honour, save in his own country"
(Matt. 13:57).

FOR THIS REASON ALONE, leaders of the Latin America Mission would have hesitated long before embarking on an Evangelism-in-Depth experiment in the LAM headquarters country of Costa Rica. But there were many other reasons to hesitate. There had been scant time to evaluate in depth the Nicaragua effort—to appraise its successes and discern its failures. There was even less time to lay the right kind of foundation in Costa Rica, and obligations in the United States would keep Strachan from participating personally in the Costa Rican effort in 1960-61. Then there were the perennial problems of funds and personnel.

Some quick efforts had indeed been made to examine the Nicaraguan program and to assess the different phases of the evangelistic effort there. Questionnaires were submitted to team members, missionaries and pastors throughout Nicaragua, to key lay leaders who had participated in one way or another. Several weeks after the close of the Managua crusade a special evaluation session was convened at which some one hundred fifty Nicaraguan leaders gathered on a Sunday afternoon to exchange their impressions as to Evangelism-in-Depth's strengths and weaknesses in Nicaragua.

As might have been expected, results varied greatly from place to place, depending upon the degree of local involvement, the enthusiasm with which the leaders threw themselves into the task, the breadth of their understanding and their commitment to Christ. When the reports were all in, however, some general observations could certainly be made.

There was no doubt that the pastors' retreat, drawing most of the Christian workers from all over Nicaragua, had been an outstanding success and had proved to be the best way of launching a national movement like Evangelism-in-Depth. Despite the inconveniences of housing and other facilities, the Holy Spirit was definitely in control of the retreat, melting hearts, deepening a prayer burden and strengthening the evangelistic conviction of all who attended. Without the healing work of the Spirit at this point in the program, it is doubtful that the movement could have attained eventual success in reaching great segments of the Nicaraguan population. It was essential that the evangelistic effort be carried on in the Spirit and not in the carnal resources of human organization and fleshly effort alone.

The sheer mechanics of coordinating simultaneous activities all over the country, of providing for the swift flow of literature, instructions and other materials to pastors, local committees, team members and others, indicated the imperative of a central office which was well organized and well staffed. Otherwise the result would have been confusion and frustration. The importance of the fortnightly newspaper, *En Marcha*, could hardly be overestimated as it brought to believers in every corner of the country up-to-date news of the movement and the coming phases of the program, providing a medium for inspiration and instruction as well as coordination of the evangelistic activities.

The visitation program was also considered to be excellent. The pattern set by John Thomas of Mexico and his committee has been followed in all subsequent Evangelism-in-Depth movements. Every city was divided and mapped; every city block, every rural hamlet, was assigned to a church. While some were more faithful in fulfilling their responsibilities than others, the net result was a tremendous onward surge of evangelistic outreach. This phase of activities was found to be the most fruitful of any single part of the total Evangelism-in-Depth program.

Such observations were rather easily made, and it was not difficult to project a similar program of activities onto the Costa Rican scene. There was pressure in this direction from all sides.

Although Evangelism-in-Depth leaders realized the need for time to reshape their strategy and think through their program, they began to wonder whether God would not have them work out their problems in the arena of evangelistic conflict rather than in an ivory tower of reflection.

The mission's Division of Evangelism was already committed to several months of activities in the part of the country where the LAM-affiliated Association of Bible Churches ministered. But this limited prospect was not sufficient to satisfy the leaders of other groups. They wanted an all-out, national effort in Costa Rica like the one in Nicaragua.

So one afternoon the fateful decision was made. Fired with hope after what they had heard and seen in Nicaragua, the national leaders of all the groups forming the Evangelical Alliance of Costa Rica overwhelmingly promised their support, enthusiasm and cooperation. When asked to stand up if they really wanted Evangelism-in-Depth, they stood as one man. The very walls seemed to vibrate as they sang "Costa Rica Shall Belong to Christ."

The mission hesitated no longer. On a somewhat more limited scale than in Nicaragua, but for better or for worse, Evangelism-in-Depth would be tried in Costa Rica.

However, the program had mushroomed and escalated unexpectedly. Leadership had to be improvised, preparations telescoped. Everything was done too quickly. Instead of a one-week pastors' retreat, a one-day conference was convened on a national holiday. While prayer cells were being formed, training classes got under way.

The Costa Rican experience clearly showed that while there had been enough time since Nicaragua to recognize the potential of Evangelism-in-Depth, more time was needed to really be able to understand the deficiencies which had been made obvious in the Nicaraguan movement and to correct these. In many instances, therefore, the Costa Rican Evangelism-in-Depth effort served only to underline or to highlight the weaknesses of Nicaragua. But this did not keep it from becoming a first-rate laboratory with opportunity for close observation and evaluation by mission leaders and other key evangelicals.

One point of improvement was the recognition that the training classes for believers should be carried on in the local church to provide a more natural framework for their learning and evangelistic experience. While this was not universally implemented in the Costa Rican effort, enough progress along these lines was made to give recognition to the need of orbiting the program around the local congregation's ministry.

This came to be an important principle of Evangelism-in-Depth. The church was envisioned as being the family in which new believers are nurtured, the cross section of the body of Christ which is to be their spiritual home, the group within which their inner life and evangelistic outreach are to be encouraged, vitalized and directed.

In keeping with the changing times in Latin America, there was a less polemic orientation in the large campaigns in Costa Rica. Instead of using an ex-priest as evangelist in the final city-wide crusade, as had been done in Nicaragua, God led the Evangelism-in-Depth leaders to invite as speaker for the San José meetings Fernando Vangioni, one of Latin America's most able preachers of the Word, a profound man of God and a silver-tongued evangelist. His morning messages each day to pastors and workers plumbed deep into the meaning of the Scriptures and the spiritual life, and the gospel message given out evening after evening was not only intellectually satisfying but emotionally compelling. Jesus Christ was presented as the crucified and resurrected Saviour—the Sinbearer and Life-giver. Men were invited to repent **and to** yield their lives to Him, their Lord and King.

Most observers agreed that had there been more time for preparation and more personnel available for ministering to the spiritual life of the believers, the result of the Costa Rican Evangelism-in-Depth effort would have been more impressive and enduring. Even so, more than 2,000 people registered their decisions for Christ during the different phases of the movement. There were at least 1,500 prayer cells unitedly seeking God's blessing; 2,444 Christians finished the training classes and cooperated in personal evangelistic efforts; and more than 50,000 homes were visited with the gospel message. Hundreds of Bible clubs for boys and girls came into being. Much of this fruit remains.

Biggest disappointment of the Evangelism-in-Depth movement in Costa Rica was the last-minute cancellation by President Mario Echandi, under direct pressure from the bishops of the Catholic Church, of the permit to parade through the streets of San José to the final closing rally of the Evangelism-in-Depth campaign.

That this could happen in an enlightened country in the year 1961 was in itself amazing. Roman Catholic spokesmen openly boasted in the newspapers that they had pressured the government into making its decision. Public reaction and newspaper comment were hot and heavy. This did nothing else at first but focus public attention on the evangelistic meetings then in progress.

The Evangelical Alliance of Costa Rica decided immediately to take the matter to the courts through what is known as a *recurso de amparo* or a legal stay.

The president **was enjoined to give cause** for his executive action, but the supreme court of the land eventually ruled in his favor, alleging that under the circumstances, and in a period several months prior to elections, a large public gathering might conceivably have occasioned a riot or other problems which he was sworn to avoid as president of the nation.

To allow this to distract Christians from their central and primary purpose of reaching the lost for Christ was Evangelism-in-Depth's gravest error. For example, while the evangelistic meeting was in progress, an impassioned caucus was held under the gymnasium grandstand at which most of the pastors and leaders of the city were trying to decide whether or not to take their case to law—this at a time when they should have been praying that the Holy Spirit would be convicting hearts and drawing men to Christ in the arena outside.

Despite every demonic intervention or human mistake, the scheduled program of Evangelism-in-Depth in Costa Rica was carried out with great enthusiasm and no little blessing. However, some grounds for wondering remained as to whether once again the emphasis had been more on breadth than on depth.

We were still experimenting, but there was no doubt in our minds that God was leading us in new and fruitful paths.

6

SPOTLIGHT ON GUATEMALA

SUNDAY, November 25, 1962, may be remembered in Guatemalan history as the date of an abortive air force revolution. But to Guatemalan Christians it was the day of the big parade.

Sunday morning began for me in the deserted downtown offices of Evangelism-in-Depth, on the top floor of a building near the post office. As the public phases of Evangelism-in-Depth were drawing to a close, the mission had sent me to Guatemala to see what had happened, and I was working on my report. We wanted answers to these questions everyone was asking: "Does Evangelism-in-Depth really work?" "Is its impact permanent?" "Does it change the churches?" "Has it been indeed a decisive struggle?" "Will it affect the course of the pattern throughout Latin America?"

We had made some bold prophecies in a folder published a year before. The folder had contained big talk—easy to predict. But did it actually happen that way? To find this out was my responsibility.

The sun was shining brightly outside the office

window. As I sifted through my notes and interview reports, I relived the previous ten hectic days in which I had met with National Coordinator Juan Isáis, visited the principal cities of the country and interviewed pastors, missionaries and laymen. In order to get an impartial picture, I—not Juan—had selected the cities and towns to be visited. Together we had driven to Jalapa, Antigua, Chimaltenango, Chichicastenango and Chiquimula. We also had chartered a light plane and flew to Quiché and Quezaltenango.

I had collected a wealth of material and I needed the quiet of a Sunday morning to organize it. Unfortunately it was a beautiful day and easy to get spring fever. It was a temptation to look out the fifth-story window and enjoy the view across the city. In the distance the grayish-green of the mountains was soothing—a peacefulness unaffected by the occasional stridency of Sunday morning traffic in the downtown street below.

Sometime in the course of my labors the persistent roar of airplanes overhead broke through my consciousness. I soon realized that they were not commercial planes and that they were not flying in fixed patterns. So I went out on the roof to take a look.

Three military fighters seemed to be taking turns at buzzing certain sections of the city. Sometimes machine-gunning could be heard and an occasional muffled roar. My own reaction, however, was to marvel at the realism of the Guatemalan Air Force on practice flights and to wonder why so many other people were out on the roofs or looking out of upper-story windows to watch the planes in action.

Not until I returned to my hotel did I find out positively that a revolution had broken out and that

President Ydígoras Fuentes was in very real danger of being overthrown. The *rat-a-tat* of machine guns, the roar of diving air force planes and the screaming of fire sirens continued to shatter the atmosphere throughout the morning. One plane was shot down. The presidential mansion was attacked. This day—of all days—a group of military officers had staged a rebellion!

Meantime, hundreds of vehicles were already converging upon the capital from all directions as evangelicals throughout the nation drove into Guatemala City to participate in Evangelism-in-Depth's concluding parade. Twenty-eight floats were ready. Signs were printed and mounted on wooden frames. Little children sported "If I get lost . . ." cards. Thousands of charts showing order and formation had been distributed.

This parade was to have been a magnificent testimony to the entire city. So now what would happen? We soon found out.

Despite the risk and the threat of a fresh attack from machine-gunning planes, and the worsening weather, Christian believers determined to give public witness to their faith in Christ. The parade, which stretched out over twenty-six blocks, went on as scheduled. Fortunately, no danger developed. The revolt was suppressed, and President Ydígoras himself arrived at the Olympic Stadium under heavy guard, submachine gun over his shoulder, cheered by the more than thirty thousand who turned out for the rally despite the tension and the intermittent rain.

Perhaps this was a typical way to conclude a typical Evangelism-in-Depth movement. Never throughout the entire year had there been assurance that the political situation would make it possible to carry the movement through to a successful culmination. The pastors' institute at the beginning of the year was held in the midst of tension and unrest as guarantees were suspended and a state of siege decreed. Throughout the following months at practically every fresh phase of the movement, a new upsurge of political strife and renewed enforcement of the curfew hour would raise the question as to whether the program of Evangelism-in-Depth should be suspended or drastically curtailed.

This was the outer conflict of those who were faced with the task of mobilizing Guatemala's 1,150 churches in a nationwide evangelistic crusade. The inner tensions and conflicts were just as real.

The decision to move ahead on the Guatemalan campaign had been postponed for five long months while the mission plowed through a slough of despair caused by fiscal deficit and the illness of its general director, Ken Strachan. Volumes of prayer went up from individuals and groups in Guatemala, in the Latin America Mission's general headquarters in Costa Rica, and elsewhere. With increasing fervor, God's servants pled for the restoring of Strachan's health and for the clearing of deficits, which would enable the mission to move forward again.

As he reflected on his own "struggles within the deep," Ken Strachan later wrote of a "never-to-be-forgotten" meeting at Keswick Grove, New Jersey, in September of 1961, when the directors of the mission and its board faced the challenge of the nationwide opportunity in Guatemala. Four million Guatemalans to be reached in cooperation with the existing evangelical forces in the course of a single year! Humanly an impossible task—so impossible that one's own body and soul faltered when faced with the decision, rendering him incapable of moving forward. In the light of staggering deficits in the preceding months, it was a hopeless proposition. Strachan recalled:

> In that moment, in the slough of doubting, God spoke to one Greatheart. A promissory note was written on a piece of scratch paper and laid before the Lord. Suddenly we were brought out of the distress of mind to the perfect haven of assurance that God would provide. From such pledges of faith and sacrificial gifts of love in moments of need throughout the long year were God's wondrous works and wonders in the deep made manifest.

Guatemala was not only the biggest and the toughest but also the "deepest" of the Evangelism-in-Depth movements to date. It was to discover this that I had driven hundreds of miles with Juan Isáis through Guatemala's breathtaking scenery, flying to the more remote corners. I taped interviews with pastors, missionaries and laymen in all parts of the country, including the capital city. I studied the careful reports compiled in the Evangelism-in-Depth office. I scanned the thousands of letters received from every corner of the republic. I attended the final crusade and the great concluding parade of Christians through the streets of Guatemala City. I talked with coordinators and team members.

The conclusion was inescapable. Guatemala had been shaken spiritually during 1962 as never before. It had been a miracle, but it was a simple fact. Throughout the year the Holy Spirit had revived churches and engendered converts in unprecedented numbers. Some fifteen thousand had made public profession of their faith in Christ.

"Just last Sunday," I was told by a missionary to the Quiché Indians, "a witch doctor—a woman—brought her magic stones and beads to Sunday school, and turning them over to the pastor, she gave a quiet testimony of how they no longer meant anything to her since Christ had come into her heart."

She was one of a dozen witch doctors converted in ʾhat town during the course of Evangelism-in-Depth, ⹂nd by her confession, she joined a great company of sinners saved by grace, as political prisoners, Jehovah's Witnesses, professional leaders, and social figures as well as many other people came to Christ.

Many conversions were spectacular. More often, however, the Spirit's work was still and deep, like the placid blue water of Lake Atitlán. Servants of God had been moved to a deeper prayer life, a more contagious witness, a more aggressive evangelism, a loving unity with Christian brethren from whom they had been estranged. Calvinists and Arminians, Dispensationalists and Pentecostals, Christians of all varieties, discovered that, as far as evangelism was concerned, they had everything important in common. They learned also that unity is a prerequisite for the most effective evangelistic impact, and that our Lord's prayer was not an idle one—"that they all may be one; . . . that the world may believe. . . ."

One preacher told me, "Although I'm a Baptist, nevertheless the fact that I have been able to have warm, cordial relationships with the other pastors . . . has helped me. It has been a magnificent experience."

"Most of the churches of our area are extremely happy about the results we are receiving in Evangelism-in-Depth," I was told by a pastor in Chimaltenango, who at first opposed the movement but later became president of the regional committee of his district. "We are planning to launch a similar movement next year to continue the job of evangelizing our country. One year just wasn't enough—the work has only begun. But Evangelism-in-Depth has set the course; it has fixed the goal; it has provided the example; and it has inspired us to forge ahead in our holy task of taking the gospel to the lost."

It was this new resolve, this new optimism, this new enthusiasm on the part of pastors and laymen that impressed me most. Like the disciples of Acts 4, many Guatemalan Christians had sought and received from the Lord boldness to speak the Word. Due to their praying together and witnessing together, the impact of the gospel had never been greater.

It took a full-time team of thirteen Latin America Mission coordinators, plus an uncounted multitude of volunteer helpers, a full year to do the job. They served as technical advisers for each phase of the Evangelism-in-Depth program.

The organizational problem was massive. A national executive committee supervised the work of thirty-two regional committees—one in each of Guatemala's district, or states, and major cities. Following the training courses for 30,000 believers (some estimates went as high as 50,000), organized house-to-house visitation took most of them on 230,000 calls, where they distributed a half million gospel portions and a million tracts.

The month of **September** saw the celebration of thirty-three cooperative regional crusades in the important cities in the republic. Each of these was characterized by a new unity among the different denominations and was climaxed by a mass parade. Fourteen hundred persons professed to accept Christ in these meetings alone.

The cost of this twelve-month project to the Latin America Mission, not including the support of the LAM missionaries, was about $70,000. In addition, most local expenditures were borne by Guatemalan Christians.

Facts like these can tell only a part of the story.

They cannot reveal the trials and agony of faith, and the spiritual struggles of Guatemalan and Latin America Mission leaders. They can never reflect the volume of intercessory prayer and sacrificial giving of God's people. The six thousand prayer-cell powerhouses in Guatemala during 1962 were unquestionably matched by many thousands of praying Christians in other parts of the world.

I realized as I wrote my report that mere statistics could never paint the picture. They could not indicate the depth of the gospel's impact, nor the extension of life-giving seed that had not yet borne fruit. Guatemalan pastors everywhere told me that they were just getting started. They said the same thing again and again—Indian pastors, whose normally stolid faces lit up with enthusiasm when they spoke of Evangelism-in-Depth—ordinarily conservative missionaries who could not suppress their excitement—Guatemalan Christians who had been fired up for the Lord as never before.

All were in agreement about the results, and their conviction became my own as I shared with them in retrospect their experiences of 1962. The year of Evangelism-in-Depth in Guatemala had ended, but Guatemala's witness and harvest had only begun.

7

TO THE ENDS OF THE EARTH

IN A SENSE, Guatemala marked the end of an era. Not only did it conclude the initial experiments of in-depth evangelism, setting the pattern for future movements, but it also was the last nationwide effort in which Ken Strachan personally was able to participate.

Preparations for the Guatemala campaign had been suspended for five months during a prolonged summer illness. But even after the green light had been given and a schedule set up, Strachan suddenly and unexpectedly succumbed to a virus infection which hospitalized him over Christmas, 1961. He was barely strong enough to attend the workers' retreat and opening meetings in Guatemala City at the end of the following January. We were to learn later that he was already suffering from Hodgkin's disease, and that a lack of resistance to virus infection is one of its symptoms.

Nevertheless, God permitted him to provide active leadership and to minister personally on a number of different occasions during the course of the exciting year of activities in the land of the quetzal. Even after the conclusion of the Guatemala effort, he directed the planning and execution of a series of seven evangelism workshops in as many different countries in Latin America in 1963, preparing the way for more extensive in-depth evangelism at a later date. The most significant of these workshops, and the only one in which Strachan himself participated, was the one held in Costa Rica, attended by key leaders from Honduras, Venezuela, Bolivia, the Dominican Republic and other parts of Latin America.

At the end of the year, a persistent lump appeared on the side of his neck, and in February a diagnosis of Hodgkin's disease required his immediate return to the United States. He was forced to cancel a visit to Honduras where Evangelism-in-Depth was approaching its climax after several months of concerted activity. Strachan spent the last year of his life in California. There, as guest professor of missions at Fuller Theological Seminary, he taught, wrote and witnessed to the urgency of the missionary task, the "inescapable calling."*

Meanwhile his colleagues in Latin America were moving ahead, implementing his ideas and the fruit of their own experience in successive Evangelism-in-Depth movements. As Evangelism-in-Depth moved from country to country, it attracted increasing interest around the world, and insistent invitations came to Ken Strachan urging him to visit Hong Kong, Japan and Taiwan to share his vision and insights with Christian leaders there. These invitations were twice deferred because of illness. Even though funds had been contributed to make possible his trip to the Orient, the

*Title under which his Fuller lectures are being published.

Lord took him Home in February, 1965, before this dream could be fulfilled.

It was a few months before his death that the General Council of the Latin America Mission was gathered at Keswick Grove in New Jersey, for a day of Bible study, prayer, and sharing of mission problems and opportunities. One of the topics under consideration was whether or not evangelicals can cooperate across a broad spectrum of denominational differences without compromising their own convictions, and how significant a part of evangelism this cooperation is.

After some discussion of the pros and cons, someone suggested that it was probably legitimate to argue pragmatically, from the success achieved by Evangelism-in-Depth and the blessing of God upon it, that its methodology was sound. After all, it was said, when John the Baptist sent his disciples to Christ to ask Him if He was the Messiah or if they should wait for another, His answer to them was an application of this pragmatic argument.

"Go and tell John," He said, "what you have seen and heard: the blind receive their sight, the lame walk, lepers are cleansed, and the deaf hear, the dead are raised up, the poor have good news preached to them" (Luke 7:22, RSV).

Therefore it seemed legitimate to recognize in the blessing of God on the Evangelism-in-Depth movement a validation of the principle of cooperation in evangelistic outreach, presuming, of course, that this principle was not contradicted in the Scriptures.

"Well, then, tell us about what the Lord has been doing in Latin America," one of the general council members said.

So, after a brief intermission, Jonás González, chief adviser of the Latin America Mission's Evangelism-in-Depth task force in Venezuela during 1964, was called into the meeting. He was asked to give an impromptu report of the moving of God's Spirit upon that country of about eight million inhabitants, with less than five hundred Protestant churches and an evangelical population of perhaps only thirty to forty thousand people.

González had been spending much time in prayer during the previous hours. He was deeply burdened for the health of Ken Strachan at that time, and was seeking God's unction for the messages he was scheduled to bring during the succeeding days at the Latin America Mission weekend conference at Keswick Grove.

It was evident from the moment he began to speak that God had put a great burden upon his heart. He seemed to be almost unconscious of his audience, and lost all sense of time, as he began very simply to tell the members of the general council what God was doing in Venezuela. He spoke of the organization of the committee structure in the geographical areas of Venezuela. He told of the 3,705 prayer cells inspired to meet regularly for prayer and witness in every part of the country. He mentioned that 18,000 lay Christians had been trained in the elementary truths of the gospel and of the Christian witness.

After the training courses had been completed, a massive door-to-door visitation campaign got under way, in which at least 300,000 Venezuelan homes were reached with a personal testimony and the gospel message in the form of a Scripture portion. González described the various special efforts that were carried on at their own expense by groups like the Soldiers of Christ from The Moody Bible Institute and the Wheaton College Band, plus local gospel teams and an exciting missionary invasion of nearly one hundred pastors, evangelists, musicians and lay workers from Puerto Rico. He told about the regional and national crusades which eventually brought the total of recorded professions of faith in Jesus Christ through Venezuela's year of Evangelism-in-Depth to 17,791.

As in his very matter-of-fact way González related these thrilling events, the men of the general council sat there, astonished at what they had heard. It was a moving report. Somehow they had not realized that God was blessing the Venezuelan effort in such degree. There was a momentary hush, but almost immediately one of them jumped to his feet.

"I feel compelled to say this," he began. "I have recently been studying the Minor Prophets, and I believe God has given me the spirit of prophecy. I seem to see a vision of Satan and his demons. One of them has come to him to report what we have just heard about Evangelism-in-Depth in Venezuela.

"Satan is furious. 'You fool!' he shouts at the demon. 'I told you two years ago in Guatemala that if something wasn't done about this, Evangelism-in-Depth would spread all over the world. Now look what's happening!'

" 'No, Sir,' the demon replies, 'we've taken care of that. We've received God's permission to touch Ken Strachan's body and he is unable to respond to invitations from other parts of the world to tell about Evangelism-in-Depth. It will not spread beyond Latin America, Sir, I assure you.'

" 'Don't be a fool!' responds Satan, 'What's the matter with his colleagues? Why can't they go?'

" 'Why, sir, we've taken care of that, too. We've sent a lying spirit to their hearts to make them think they are too busy.' " And the speaker sat down.

There was a stunned silence for a few seconds. Then the president of the board broke into Spirit-led prayer. The Holy Ghost came upon the gathering, and one after another all thirty men led in prayer, with tears and confession and with intercession for Ken Strachan, for Venezuela, and for Evangelism-in-Depth around the world. Only God knows what victories were won in those two hours of Spirit-led praying.

After that experience it was impossible for Rubén Lores and me to say no when a year later, after the home-going of Ken Strachan, we were asked to make the trip which his poor health had made impossible for him to take. It was felt that as a mission we should respond to the insistent invitation of missionary leaders in the Far East to share with them some of the Latin American experience and God's blessing upon Evangelism-in-Depth in this part of the world.

So, on February 6, 1966, with a minimum of preparation and with very little idea of what lay ahead, the two of us took off from Seattle to Tokyo, Japan, on the first leg of a concentrated six-week tour of areas in Asia and the Mediterranean where special interest in Evangelism-in-Depth had been evidenced.

We got off on the wrong foot by forgetting to take the international date line into account. As a result we failed to arrive on schedule for an all-day seminar of pastors in Tokyo! Fortunately our hosts were creative and, through the use of a local speaker and Evangelism-in-Depth filmstrips, improvised a better program than perhaps we ourselves could have presented. They were also charitable and forgave our stupid oversight. We told them they were inadvertently implementing one of the basic principles of Evangelism-in-Depth—that the program must be carried on by local rather than by imported leaders!

To visit fourteen new countries in forty-four days can be an overwhelming experience even for seasoned tourists. But in our case, added to the normal sights, sounds, conversations and impressions was a schedule of sixteen seminars, lasting from three to twelve hours each, plus about thirty lectures and sermons. It is easy to imagine the difficulties Rubén Lores and I had as we attempted to sift down our reactions into intelligent and significant conclusions!

In the first place, there was consistently more interest than expected in Evangelism-in-Depth. We received a warmer welcome than we had anticipated or deserved on such an unstructured and improvised trip. The turnout for seminars and meetings was generally well above local expectations. We could only interpret this as a genuine interest in Evangelism-in-Depth, or at least a groping for some more hopeful patterns of evangelism in non-growth areas. In either case, it was gratifying and promised to become a hopeful starting-off place.

Our second general impression was the similarities we encountered in each of the nations visited. Everywhere the evangelical church is in a minority situation. In almost every country we could see repeated—like carbon copies—the same sterile patterns of church structure, the same failure to focus either on the *evan-*

71

gelistic mission of the church or on *the church* as God's evangelistic missioner, the same staggering percentages of children and young people on the streets and in the church largely ignored by mission strategists, the same freedom and unlimited opportunities for preaching the gospel, the same encouraging responsiveness when it is adequately communicated, together with the same difficulties in communication, the same interdenominational tensions (stronger in U.S.-oriented mission fields than in British- or European-oriented ones), and even the same desire to try Evangelism-in-Depth.

As we moved into a country and had opportunity to speak to pastors, students, and missionaries, our "message" covered from one to five topics:

1. The "why" of our trip. We told something about the work of God's Spirit in Evangelism-in-Depth in Latin America, our privileged position as observers, the worldwide interest that had arisen in six short years, Ken Strachan's invitations, and the provision for this trip through a Christian foundation and the R. Kenneth Strachan Memorial Fund for World Evangelism.

2. The principles of in-depth evangelism. With some subsequent development and modification, we followed the outline of a flip-chart prepared just before our departure, in which the major principles were represented as the four columns of a temple. However, a blackboard turned out to be the best medium for communicating these principles in what was basically a classroom context.

3. The program of Evangelism-in-Depth. Depending on the available time, we developed the implemen-

tation of the in-depth principles in a specific program, touching not only on the common factors but also on the "attitude" of Evangelism-in-Depth, so essential to the success of the movement.

4. The history of how Evangelism-in-Depth developed. Only in full-day seminars or where no translation was required (which made it possible to cover more territory) were we able to get to this topic.

5. Nonstatistical implications, results, projections or secondary dimensions of Evangelism-in-Depth. Rubén Lores had seventeen points in this lecture, but never got beyond the sixth point for lack of time! This is a very important area, however, and was usually covered at least in part through discussion and questions and answers.

We quickly became aware of the need for either prolonged or multiple exposure if we were adequately to communicate the basic concepts of Evangelism-in-Depth. A full-day seminar (and hence at least a two-man team) seemed almost essential. In situations where full-day seminars were not set up, the Lord allowed us to travel together with key individuals, and multiple exposure became a satisfactory substitute for (or maybe even better than) prolonged exposure. The principles of Evangelism-in-Depth are really quite simple and biblical and not difficult to get across. But the implications of these principles are endless and need time to sink in.

The second major purpose of our trip was to learn about evangelistic methods and experiments in other lands, and particularly to find out what we could about the experiments inspired by Evangelism-in-Depth. We discovered that in the countries we visited there have been nine or ten such experiments. They are as follows:

Japan—a cooperative effort in the Chichibu Valley involving about a dozen churches and three denominations.

Korea—Nationwide Evangelistic Campaign in 1965. Final reports were not in yet at the time of our visit.

Taiwan—Kaohsiung area—sponsored by Overseas Crusades and still going on during our stopover.

Philippines—Christ for Greater Manila Crusade, still going on.

Indonesia—Bandung, city-wide, pre-Pentecost evangelistic campaign, just getting under way—the first cooperative evangelistic campaign in the history of Java's second largest city. Also in Indonesia, a successful experiment in prayer-cell witness sparked by Mac Bradshaw.

Thailand—an inter-faith evangelism committee had emerged from two retreats on evangelism and was definitely planning an Evangelism-in-Depth movement.

India—seven denominations had just completed a two-year program of in-depth evangelism in the northern part of the state of Maharashtra. We were present for final reports and evaluation.

Lebanon—a provisional steering committee was successfully enlisting support for a nationwide Evangelism-in-Depth movement and communicating the in-depth principles.

Portugal—an "Office for the Promotion of Evangelism" was looking forward to a national movement of Evangelism-in-Depth. At their invitation, Juan Isáis visited Portugal a few months later for additional workshops.

It was a privilege to see and hear of these efforts. Our hearts were encouraged, and many of the evangelistic insights and techniques we observed may find application in Latin America. There was much that we could not see. For example, we were unable to visit Africa, where Nigeria's "New Life For All" movement has been pioneering in-depth principles with conspicuous success. But the examples mentioned serve at least to indicate the extent of interest in Evangelism-in-Depth and the need for more adequate and careful sharing of experiences.

In general it can be said that in the areas visited the information available about our Latin American experiments had been woefully inadequate. Comprehension of the principles of in-depth evangelism was generally limited and correctives needed to be applied. We felt at the time that there was much which our Asian and European brethren could perhaps learn from Latin America. But we were also very conscious that the Spirit of God is at work in the lands we visisted. He is leading Christians into creative experiments. The tables may soon be reversed. Latin America may soon be on the receiving end. If so, we need to establish channels of communication and sharing for our own sakes in Latin America as well as for the greater objectives of world evangelism. Already in-depth evangelism in Africa has developed phenomenally, and other parts of the world could profit greatly from the new patterns emerging in Nigeria and the Congo.

We discovered that the Latin American has a distinct advantage over the North American in communicating to Asians and Europeans. The fact that Evangelism-in-Depth comes from a "younger church" gives it much more prestige than if it were a U.S. export. The fact that Latin Americans are its spokesmen also helps. Regardless of the role in communication played by North American missionaries—and this must perhaps be a large one, due to the necessity of using English rather than Spanish overseas—the major load of basic communication can best be carried by Latin Americans.

Again and again we were impressed at how wonderfully the Lord undertook in the details of travel, particularly in getting us into places where we did not realize we should go and in keeping us out of places we had intended to visit!

In Bangkok, for example, where we had planned to stop off for only twenty-four hours just to see the city, we discovered a very keen, interdenominational committee which represented the entire evangelical community and which was planning Evangelism-in-Depth for Thailand. At their last meeting they had circulated what little information they had—the book, *Evangelism-in-Depth,* and some pamphlets. And they had promised to read up on Evangelism-in-Depth before their next session. We arrived between those two meetings and on a Saturday, when the men were free to meet with us for most of the day! We did not or could not have planned it. God did.

Likewise, through a temporary juggling of plane schedules, God kept us out of Southern India under what we later learned would have been the wrong sponsorship! These are only two illustrations of the ways in which our Lord watched over us. There were many, many more. We could only thank Him, and also His people for their prayers.

We returned home exhilarated and awed by what we had seen of the working of God's Spirit and the potential that stretched ahead into the future. Rubén Lores wrote:

> As we look back on the varied experiences of this trip, one overall impression keeps coming back to us. Everywhere we went we saw multitudes of people. Discerning Christians have "lifted up their eyes" and have seen that "the fields are already white unto harvest." They are praying the Lord of the harvest to send forth laborers into His harvest, and He will not fail them. The Christians in Japan, Thailand, Lebanon and Portugal are a tiny minority, but they are convinced that a dedicated minority can make an impact on a whole nation.
>
> The next few years may well be the greatest years of ingathering from many nations, as has happened already in seven Latin-American countries. Christians can work together in evangelism, and when they do, God can work miracles to accomplish His purpose.

8

SLINGS AND ARROWS

VIEWING IN RETROSPECT the development of Evangelism-in-Depth, one is tempted to think that it would have been so much easier if God had revealed a complete set of principles and guidelines, and then had simply commanded His servants to implement them. But there was no Mount Sinai and no tables of stone.

Patterns were necessarily quite different in each country. Much depended on the available resources and the development of the work to date. For example, in Guatemala the skills and experiences of Youth for Christ International, with their missionaries and their "Teen Teams," were available to us, whereas the Honduras Evangelism-in-Depth movement could count on no specialized help in this area. The problems, needs and available resources made the picture so different in each area that it was not easy to detect the common principles on which the program was based.

Evangelism-in-Depth thus did not first emerge as a full-blown theory which was then put into practice. It has been rather a cumulative experience of God's people in different countries, from which, as observers and participants, we have tried to draw inferences and to extract principles. One thing was clear: God was at work. And it was evident that, despite human limitations and inadequate experience, Evangelism-in-Depth held great promise for the twentieth century church.

Mistakes, nevertheless, were frequent, and trial and error revealed many deficiencies of the program and of our understanding of its philosophy. Constructive criticism has always played an important role in the development of Evangelism-in-Depth.

The criticism begins "at home." After each national movement the personnel of the Latin America Mission's Division of Evangelism holds exhaustive and merciless evaluation sessions, seeking to analyze the strengths and the weaknesses of the program. Team members have learned to overcome personal resentments and subjective judgments as in frankness they have exposed deficiencies in approach and activities. Close associates, such as George Sánchez of The Navigators, have helped us to see the dangers of slipping into the simpler patterns of traditional mass evangelism. Others have pointed out the need in Latin America for an adequate context of social concern in evangelistic preaching. In particular, the debate carried on in the columns of the *International Review of Missions* by Kenneth Strachan and Victor Hayward has contributed not only a sharper focus on theological presuppositions, but also a more theologically adequate articulation of principles. Evangelism-in-Depth had often been described in terms more methodological than scriptural.

As in apostolic days, dissension between Christians

has frequently been the greatest obstacle to effective evangelism. In Guatemala, at the very height of the Evangelism-in-Depth activity, one of the major denominations suffered a serious internal schism that was in no way related to the movement. The split distracted the attention of leaders as well as of the rank and file of that particular denomination. It was impossible for them to cooperate fully. And they did not reap as many benefits as they otherwise might have.

Another schism tarnished the fellowship of Christians in Honduras, just as Evangelism-in-Depth was getting under way. The largest mission, under isolationist pressures, withdrew its collaboration from the nationwide movement and launched its own parallel program.

More recently, in Bolivia, on the day following the conclusion of the formal Evangelism-in-Depth program, a letter was sent out inviting churches to form a new Evangelical Fellowship which excluded some of the major denominations with whom the signers of the letter had been working harmoniously during the Evangelism-in-Depth effort. This type of division is deplored by Latin America Mission leaders and causes them great concern.

These clashes, of course, have not been occasioned by Evangelism-in-Depth itself. In Bolivia the tension was longstanding, and was simply held off to insure the fulfillment of Evangelism-in-Depth's program. Nor are such splits the general rule. In other countries pastoral retreats and other activities of Evangelism-in-Depth have been used of God to heal divisions and to reconcile Christians. This was notably true in the pastors' institutes in Nicaragua and Venezuela.

Unfortunately, there are times when, as soon as Evangelism-in-Depth is over, old feuds reassert themselves and narrowness of outlook again restricts the ample working of the Spirit of God. Blaming any resurgence of bigotry on Evangelism-in-Depth, however, is like accusing the food one ate yesterday of making him hungry today! We need to be thankful, at least, that yesterday we were well fed, or by analogy, united in our witness to Christ.

Apart from any marginal attacks from either the extreme right or the extreme left, it seems to us that most of the honest criticism of Evangelism-in-Depth stems from the following misconceptions: (1) a false conception of the structure of Evangelism-in-Depth, which makes it easy to look in the wrong direction for results; (2) an inadequate understanding of the objectives of Evangelism-in-Depth, which makes it easy to look for the wrong kind of results; and (3) an unscriptural posture within the body of Christ.

1. *A false conception of the structure of Evangelism-in-Depth.* Often it is assumed that Evangelism-in-Depth is an imported program, and observers tend to blame the imbalance of outreach or lack of results in any one phase or activity upon the visiting advisers or upon the movement itself. Questions like these are raised: Why did Evangelism-in-Depth not get directly involved in the Dominican crisis? Why is Evangelism-in-Depth not more deeply involved with social problems? Why is it simplistic and individualistic? Or, from another sector, why were there not more conversions in *our* denomination?

First, it should perhaps be repeated that the program of Evangelism-in-Depth varies greatly from country

to country. Basically it is an effort to match all the
available resources of the evangelical community—
men, money, methods, means—against the needs and
opportunities for witness and evangelism. Since both
these and the resources vary greatly, so does the program. While gaps can sometimes be filled in part by
outside help, there will always be varying strengths
and weaknesses in the program of any given country.

The program thus is the program of the local, national Christian community, reflecting its own particular vision, vigor and shortcomings. Naturally, the
"advisers" who make up the Latin America Mission
team in a given country have opportunity to enlarge
the vision and planning of the local leaders. As technical consultants this is their job. But the process of
inspiration and education is a protracted one. Often
it is impossible within the limitations of time to incul-
cate or to implement all the ideas and projects which
might be desirable. Any lack of social concern, for
example, would more likely be a reflection of the de-
ficiency of the entire evangelical community or of its
inadequate resources along these lines than of Evangelism-in-Depth itself.

In point of fact, however, local leaders of Evangelism-in-Depth have been alert to the opportunities for
social service. The Bolivia movement included a very
extensive program of literacy, headed by ALFALIT
personnel. Although the Dominican Republic has a
higher literacy rate than Bolivia, there was a great deal
of activity along these lines in connection with the
movement there as well.

In several Evangelism-in-Depth efforts, "Goodwill
Caravans" have dramatized the evangelical responsi-

bility to the whole man, as doctors, nurses, agronomists and others moved into the rural areas to minister in the name of Christ. In all of this Evangelism-in-Depth has sought to emphasize social concern, but always placing it within the context of evangelism rather than of philanthropy, and thus making it distinctly Christian and Christlike.

Criticism of Evangelism-in-Depth for not being sufficiently involved in the revolution in the Dominican Republic is superficial. Alejandro Paniagua, a non-evangelical editorialist of the daily newspaper, *Listín Diario,* was so impressed by the constructive efforts of Evangelism-in-Depth to reduce hatred and violence and to promote goodwill and morality, that he devoted three consecutive editorials to what is an almost embarrassing eulogy of the evangelicals and of the Evangelism-in-Depth program. He calls the evangelicals "the true revolutionaries," those who are concerned with the reconstruction of the Dominican soul, the all-important ethical and human values and the spiritual orientation that a nation like the Dominican Republic needs in its hour of political darkness.

On the human level the success of Evangelism-in-Depth in the Dominican Republic was due first and foremost to the indomitable spirit and courage of the advisers and coordinators who, by their very presence in the midst of difficulty and danger, demonstrated the depth and reality of their concern for the welfare of the Dominican people, regardless of any particular political alignment.

Sometimes criticism of Evangelism-in-Depth comes from pastors or churches who have failed to become really involved in the program and therefore have not reaped benefits in the same degree as the other denominations or churches who have given themselves wholeheartedly to the evangelistic task. The scriptural axiom still holds true: "He who sows sparingly will reap sparingly, and he who sows bountifully will also reap bountifully" (II Cor. 9:6, RSV). When the true structure of Evangelism-in-Depth is understood, then observers will look to the local church to determine its effectiveness. This effectiveness, in turn, will depend directly upon the degree of involvement and activity demonstrated in that church.

2. *An inadequate understanding of the objectives of Evangelism-in-Depth.* Frequently we find that students of Evangelism-in-Depth are looking for the wrong kind of results because they do not understand the true objectives of Evangelism-in-Depth. They are concerned only about new members and new faces. These are important; it would be wrong to affirm otherwise. The purpose of evangelism is to produce new converts, and it has been our experience that when the right methods and principles are used, the Lord does honor them with conversions.

But immediate church growth is not the only positive result which should be expected from a large-scale Evangelism-in-Depth effort. The new spirit of faith, courage and optimism on the part of the Dominican people as they discovered that not even war or revolution could thwart God's evangelistic purpose through His church was exciting. This new zeal, this new enthusiasm, this new boldness to speak the Word of God, is difficult to measure, but it is one of the most significant products of an Evangelism-in-Depth effort.

Allen Thompson, field director of the West Indies Mission, wrote:

Twelve months ago hopes for triumph seemed scant. At the close of the first EID pastors' retreat at the WIM center in La Vega, chilling announcements of a bloody revolution's outbreak filled the air. These reports stated: "A military coup has taken over the government! Shooting and bombing have broken out on the streets of Santo Domingo."

Revolution! Would this be the death knell to gospel endeavor? Could our heart longings and prayers for revival be realized in a nation at civil war? On the other hand, has the Church of Jesus Christ nothing to offer to downtrodden people seeking solutions to dire living conditions, illiteracy, exploitation, poverty? Does the gospel change only the soul of man, or can we see it revolutionizing the home, the job, the nation? The little band of workers—Dominican Christians, missionaries, and EID personnel— declared themselves in favor of identification for Christ's sake with the people and their problems. The ominous circumstances of the revolution would be utilized, not shunned. As one of the Latin leaders, Juan Isáis, put it: "This is the time to strike. The spirit of action in a revolution is the spirit of growth."

So, in stormy days and with the pounding of gunfire about them, soldiers of the Cross began to penetrate with the gospel a country that was destined for spiritual renaissance. . . . That this mission was accomplished during a bitter revolution demonstrates the spirit and responsibility of a revived Church.*

*"Power in Midst of Peril," *Whitened Harvest,* July-August, 1966, p. 6f.

If in his report Thompson had chosen to include statistical proof of God's blessing during Evangelism-in-Depth on the island he might have mentioned what he wrote in another article about the growth of his own mission. He stated:

> In 1939 the West Indies Mission began work in the Dominican Republic, a country which soon proved to be almost impenetrable to the Gospel. The 27 years of difficult sowing in tears yielded 15 congregations and around 900 believers in Christ. In the year of evangelism just past, the reaping in joy has added to the WIM effort 2 churches, 8 additional preaching points, and approximately 700 new believers."†

A few years ago the secretary of the Bible Society for Central America described the churches of his area as "tired." Now the situation has changed dramatically as in many cases they have moved from a stagnant into a growth situation. This is the subtle but significant change toward which we are striving—a collective experience on the part of the whole body of Christ, wherein discouragement turns to hopefulness, negativism to optimism, indifference to aggressiveness, doubt to faith, and timidity to courage. The experience of Acts 4 is one of Evangelism-in-Depth's basic objectives, as by God's grace and the work of the Holy Spirit, patterns of stagnancy are replaced by patterns of growth in the Christian community.

Evangelism-in-Depth also produces new leadership on every level. Denominational leaders become national leaders; local pastors and workers become effective denominational planners and executives; raw and

†Thompson, "Points to Ponder," *Whitened Harvest*, July-August, 1966, p. 8.

untrained members of the local church emerge into positions of leadership and responsibility they had not previously experienced. Evangelism-in-Depth is a yearlong school of evangelism of which the training of leadership is a highly significant by-product.

In Venezuela the new secretary of the Bible Society, an engineer, proved his worth as a lay leader of the Evangelism-in-Depth visitation program before he was tapped for his present position. Another Venezuelan, a Baptist pastor, showed unexpected abilities in the field of journalism and promotion, making him the logical choice of his denomination to head the promotion of a follow-up program of evangelism the next year. This sort of thing occurs everywhere.

Evangelism-in-Depth likewise produces candidates for the Christian ministry, child evangelism teachers, literacy workers, visitors and personal workers, administrators and committee leaders, prayer warriors, stewards, preachers, evangelists, organizers, teachers, promoters. It encourages Christian stewardship. It provides opportunities for partnership between missions and national churches, missionaries and local leaders. It introduces new methods and techniques and imparts skills that have previously been untried.

"Goodwill Caravans" and ALFALIT literacy projects have broken new ground in several countries. Evangelism-in-Depth activities have widened horizons and increased vision, adding new dimensions of social concern and personal witness to the preaching of the gospel. Spiritual growth and Christian maturity are accelerated. Therefore, the spiritual returns and intangible fruit go far beyond the mere statistics of public response to the preaching of the gospel. The movement must be evaluated on the basis of these intangibles and indirect by-products, as well as on the basis of direct results and statistics.

3. By far the greatest number of criticisms that come to us derive from what we consider to be *an unscriptural posture within the body of Christ*. Evangelism-in-Depth is accused of being "ecumenism in depth" by right-wingers, but critics from the left accuse it of narrow fundamentalism! It has been blamed by some for being too soft on Romanism, and by others of being too polemic in its anti-Roman stance. These and many other criticisms stem from wrong understandings of the kinship within the body of Christ which should govern our attitudes and intra-Christian relations.

Most of us would agree that our unity in the body of Christ, as it is expounded in the Scriptures, is *positional*. That is, it is based upon our common relationship to Christ, the Head. As Christians we all have a common source of life, a common source of spiritual sustenance, a common relationship to God. The classical passages of the body of Christ—Romans 12, I Corinthians 10 and 12, Ephesians 4—all make this clear.

This relationship, of course, is not of our own making. It is a *de facto* situation, imposed on us by the redemptive, re-creative act of God in our salvation. St. Paul is careful to point out, therefore, that since it is not of our own making, we cannot dissolve it!

The ear cannot say, Paul affirms to the Corinthians, "Because I am not the eye, I am not of the body," and thus withdraw into the limbo of unrelatedness. There is no secession from the body of Christ.

On the other hand, "the eye cannot say unto the hand"—nor the Baptist to the Pentecostal—"I have no need of thee" (I Cor. 12:16,21). No individual member has the right to exclude anyone else whom the Spirit of God has borne into the family of God, the body of Christ. Spiritual *apartheid* is equally unscriptural.

This positional unity has been secured for us by a common experience which Paul describes in its several dimensions in Ephesians 4:1-6:

> I therefore, a prisoner for the Lord, beg you to lead a life worthy of the calling to which you have been called, with all lowliness and meekness, with patience, forbearing one another in love, eager to maintain the unity of the Spirit in the bond of peace. There is one body and one Spirit, just as you were called to the one hope that belongs to your call, one Lord, one faith, one baptism, one God and Father of us all, who is above all and through all and in all (Ephesians 4:1-6 RSV).

There is one *Spirit*, who engendered us. This is the soteriological dimension of our experience. Ours is a common *hope* of eternal union with Christ, which is our experience in its eschatological dimension.

The existential dimension of our experience is defined in our common *Lord*, who is our Master, and our common *faith*, or response to His call. The sacramental dimension is seen in our common *baptism*, which is the sign of identification with Christ. The outward form or symbolism of baptism may differ, but it represents a common dimension of the Christian experience in the simple fact that it is a sign of our allegiance to Christ— to each of us a means of grace and witness. Finally, Paul tells the Ephesians that in its theological dimen-

89

sion our common experience relates to one *God and Father*, the Source of our common life.

There is a sort of finality about this positional unity of ours in Christ that should make us afraid to tamper with it. Differences between brothers may be numerous, but the relationship is permanent. I may be compelled at times even to reprove my brother in Christ, but when I fail to acknowledge him as my brother, how that must grieve the Father's heart!

Again, the Scriptures seem to underline the truth that the unity of the body is *functional*. Paul glories in its diversity of gifts, of callings, of offices. They seem to roll off his tongue: apostles, prophets, evangelists, pastors, teachers, helpers, administrators, the utterance of wisdom and of knowledge, faith, healing, miracles, prophecy, discernment, tongues, interpretation of tongues, and so forth.

But as he mentions them, the apostle always makes the central point that the members contribute to the edification of the whole, to the preparation of the saints for the ministry of the gospel, to the health and function of the total body of Christ. The fact is, we need each other. From the very beginning, it has been our Lord's intention that His body should act *as a body*, not as a haphazard, uncoordinated collection of limbs and members!

In the city of Seoul, Korea, we visited a therapeutic center for young spastics. There we saw therapists strapping boards to the feet of small children to help them walk. We watched the children struggle, with the help of braces, walkers and crutches, to get around the room. Eating also presented its problems, and racks had been developed to help them get their spoons to their mouths. All these efforts were required just to fulfill the most normal functions of life—because their limbs were not coordinated.

How similar to the church of Christ, we thought. How long will it continue to shuffle across the stage of human history like the uncoordinated victim of cerebral palsy? God wants the body of Christ to be a *body*—a healthy body, a functioning body—to do the work which He commended to it in the great, universal commission.

The unity we seek is centered primarily in the proclamation of the gospel. It is a unity of witness, and a united testimony may be given in ways that require very little organizational involvement. A plan of evangelistic activities that calls for two churches to do house-to-house visitation in different sections of the city at the same time does not imply a merger of the two groups or any compromise of their respective doctrines. In fact, Evangelism-in-Depth might as accurately be called simultaneous evangelism as cooperative evangelism. Somehow, despite differences, we must learn to love each other, pray for each other, pray with each other, and work together for the glory of Christ and the extension of His gospel.

This bridge-building attitude, as much as the unity of our witness, provides for successful communication of the gospel of Christ to the unbelieving world beyond us. As we love each other, it is easier to love the nonbeliever. As we pray for each other, it is easier to pray together for the unsaved.

Beyond the positional and functional unity of the body of Christ, its oneness is also *visible*. Many Christians will balk at this concept, but it seems to be the clear import of our Lord's high priestly prayer in John 17. The unity of the disciples is to be the silent witness, the seal and confirmation of their message, the means by which the unbelieving world may know Him, whom to know aright is life eternal. And if the world is to be impressed by this unity, it must be able to see it in the visible life of the church.

"I do not pray for these only," Jesus said, "but also for those who believe in me through their word, that they may all be one; even as thou, Father, art in me, and I in thee, that they also may be in us, so that the world may believe that thou hast sent me" (John 17:20-21, RSV).

We who are in the family of God may recognize those large basic truths which we hold in common, and distinguish them from the lesser, secondary doctrines and practices that set us apart from each other as Christians. But to the unbeliever who stands outside the miracle of God's grace in Christ, there is nothing so confusing as what appears to be a sectarian preaching of Christ. He does not distinguish between the important and the secondary, the large and the small. "Invisible" unity is precisely that—invisible!

Denominational emphases are important, and we need them. Each is a corrective for the other. We are not advocating mergers, nor erasures of distinctives. But, very simply, we need each other, and the unbelieving world needs our common gospel.

Evangelism-in-Depth always tries to emphasize the tremendous importance of the unity of the body of Christ to our common life and ministry—sometimes against overwhelming pressures. We insist that for the sake of Christ and the gospel and the unbelieving world, we need to proclaim together, at least occasionally, what we believe together. Seen in this context, Christian cooperation in evangelism is not optional but obligatory.

This posture, which we believe is scriptural, has often been criticized by fellow Christians. But the Latin America Mission's team of technical advisers learned to live with criticism as they moved from Guatemala to Honduras, to Venezuela, and then to Bolivia and the Dominican Republic. This was part of the developing and maturing process of the movement. Through this means a more clearly defined, more lucidly articulated, and more effectively implemented Evangelism-in-Depth could come to be a truly significant part of contemporary church history in Latin America and around the world.

9

RETHINKING EVANGELISM—
EVANGELISM-IN-DEPTH
PRINCIPLES

THE YEARS since Ken Strachan and Juan Isáis first experimented in Nicaragua have left their impact on the development of in-depth concepts of evangelism. Dialogue with Christian leaders from other continents and other ecclesiastical frameworks, experience in the front lines of evangelism in a constantly increasing number of areas, the barbs of critics and the plaudits of friends, together with a deeper understanding of what God's Word has to tell us—these factors and the response to them have demonstrated that Evangelism-in-Depth is a dynamic concept. It is a movement of the Spirit of God upon the hearts of His people—a revival in motivation and methodology.

Nor has the articulation of its principles been static. Different situations require different explanations, and a variety of response calls for an evolution of presentation. Time and experience have underscored the importance of some elements of the program which at first seemed incidental, and vice versa.

Evangelism-in-Depth is constantly growing. The program is frequently modified, and the articulation of its principles, varied. However, under the changes of form and expression the fundamental theorem first stated by Kenneth Strachan remains the same: "The growth of any movement is in direct proportion to the success of that movement in mobilizing its total membership in the constant propagation of its beliefs." This theorem has given direction to the development of Evangelism-in-Depth as it strives to renew, motivate, and mobilize Christians, pushing its roots deep into the devotional life, intra-church relationships, and outward witness of each individual believer—adult, youth, child, illiterate, student or professional.

Traditional evangelism centers in the evangelist. Every effort is made to increase the breadth of his ministry, to enlarge his audience, to multiply his hearers. Evangelism-in-Depth does not deny the validity of this purpose. On the contrary, it encourages it, but its thrust is different. Instead of trying to multiply the number of hearers, Evangelism-in-Depth tries to multiply the number of witnesses. It does this by helping every Christian believer to participate in the evangelistic thrust of the Christian church.

The basic flaw in the traditional evangelistic campaign method does not exist in what it does, but what it cannot do. It is only one side of the coin. It is the expression of the charismatic *evangelistic gift*, but in its customary application it is not adequately related to the universal *evangelistic responsibility* of the body of Christ, all of whose members are called to be witnesses. It is geared to the outreach of the professional, but is not ordinarily structured to involve fully the layman. It **achieves** "breadth" in the proclamation of the gospel. It fails to secure "depth" in the personal experience and participation of every Christian believer.

There is no disputing the ultimate objective of the evangelistic task. It is clearly stated in the five versions of our Lord's universal or Great Commission as recorded for us by Matthew, Mark and John in their gospels, and by Luke in his gospel and the book of the Acts. In each case the charge is given to a slightly different group of disciples and sometimes on different occasions. In all probability Jesus repeated the same message many times in different forms and contexts. This was the burden of His ministry to the disciples between His resurrection and His ascension. He took advantage of every opportunity to impress them with their responsibility and privilege as witnesses to Him and to His finished work of redemption. These passages simply summarize the essential message of His forty-day ministry among them.

The objective, then, is to take the good news to all the world, to all nations, to all creatures, and to proclaim it so that all can hear and understand and be fairly challenged to accept the gift of new life in Christ. This gospel must be preached in its full ethical context—"teaching them to observe all that I have commanded you"—as well as in its sacramental implications —"baptizing them in the name of the Father and of the Son and of the Holy Spirit"—and above all in the supernatural power of the Spirit—"stay in the city until you are clothed with power from on high."

The Great Commission carries other significant overtones. For example, the command to "disciple the nations" in Matthew 28:19 (marginal rendering) could be exegeted to imply the need of a witness to the social and political structures in which sinful men find themselves in spiritual need. A degree of social concern is certainly reflected in the response to the Great Commission which the apostles and disciples themselves exhibited in the book of Acts.

Nevertheless, the broad lines of the objective are clear, and among professional evangelists there are no serious differences of interpretation. This was evident in the remarkable unity of heart and mind shared by virtually all the delegates to the 1966 World Congress on Evangelism in Berlin. The goal is the total penetration of the world with the gospel of Christ.

Traditional evangelism recognizes this objective and zeros in on it with commendable zeal and effectiveness. It has seen the ultimate objective. Yet it has often failed to discern the penultimate step. "If our goal is the penetration of the whole world," observes Leighton Ford, "then for the *agents* to carry out this task we must aim at nothing less than the *mobilization of the whole Church.*"*

He goes on to make this strong, but fully documentable, statement: "A church which bottlenecks its outreach by depending on its specialists—its pastors or evangelists—to do its witnessing, is living in violation of both the intention of its Head and the consistent pattern of the early Christians."†

Christ never intended to leave evangelism exclusively to the apostles. In Acts 8, when the Christians

The Christian Persuader (New York: Harper & Row, 1966), p. 45.
†*Ibid.*, p. 46.

97

were persecuted and dispersed, their experience was described in these terms: "A great persecution arose against the church in Jerusalem; and they were all scattered throughout the region of Judea and Samaria, *except* the apostles. Now those who were scattered went about preaching the word" (Acts 8:1,4, RSV).

Clearly, the church bears a universal responsibility to evangelistic witness—laity and clergy alike—beyond the professional ministry of those gifted for leadership. Ephesians 4 would seem to teach that the leadership is thus gifted for the purpose of mobilizing the church.

The failure of traditional evangelistic efforts to emphasize this penultimate objective of mobilizing the church in evangelistic witness is the most serious criticism that can be leveled against it. Yet the failure here is not on the part of the evangelist. He is faithfully and effectively exercising the gift God has given him. The failure is on the part of the church which does not recognize its own universal obligation to witness and to act—as was Christ's intention—as the agent for penetrating the entire world with the gospel of salvation.

"The mobilization of the Church will call for a drastic revolution," Ford rightly predicts, "in the relation of the clergy and the laity. For too long the accepted pattern was: the layman *pays* the minister to evangelize and to do the whole work of the ministry. Then the growth of lay organization in the churches led to another pattern: the layman *helps* the clergy to evangelize and minister. This was a welcome advance, but still fell short of the New Testament ideal, . . .

"In terms of evangelism, the old pattern will not do. It is not enough for the layman to *pay* the preacher to win souls, **or even** *help* him to do so. The pattern is that *the minister helps the layman* to evangelize!"‡

Many would agree that this is the New Testament ideal, but they would throw up their hands and say, "It can't be done!"

Evangelism-in-Depth in Latin America has an answer to that attitude. It simply responds, "It *has* been done. God has done it. The churches have been mobilized. Evangelism-in-Depth is now a part of the church history of more than seven nations!"

It has been successfully demonstrated that when the Spirit of God moves upon His people to give them a collective sense of burden and urgency, they *can* be mobilized in all-out evangelism. Earnest Christians in Nicaragua, Costa Rica, Guatemala, Honduras, Venezuela, Bolivia, the Dominican Republic and Peru have learned by experience that abundant sowing *can* bring abundant harvest. They have discovered that Christians *can* work together in evangelism, their fellowship scaling the barriers of racial and creedal idiosyncrasies to "build bridges" among themselves and to the unbelieving world they are anxious to reach for Jesus Christ.

Their experience has been akin to that of the disciples who hesitantly placed the little lad's loaves and fishes in Christ's hands, only to discover that paucity of resources is no problem for Him. When resources are pooled and surrendered, they are enough for the task, because in the Lord's hands they are touched by miracle.

Evangelism-in-Depth in Latin America is not really

‡*Ibid.*, pp. 47-49.

a "program," although its principles are clear and essential. It is more correctly a "phenomenon"—a collective experience of God's grace and power, a laboratory in which God's Spirit can perform a mighty act and demonstrate to the rest of the world that God is *not* dead, the task *can* be accomplished, the church *can* be mobilized, and the New Testament method is *not* outdated.

Generally in Latin America it has taken from two to five years for a country to "gird itself" for Evangelism-in-Depth. Christians cannot be mobilized unless there is a measure of expectancy throughout the membership of the church. Pastors must be willing for the kind of revolution in clergy-laity relationships to which Leighton Ford refers. Key leaders must be burdened for evangelism.

Whether it be through pastors' retreats, revival services, or evangelism workshops, eventually there comes a time when the Spirit of God seems to be saying to everybody, "Now! Now is the accepted time!" When this collective experience of readiness to believe and to obey becomes discernible in the church, Evangelism-in-Depth can become a realizable objective.

Mobilization is the key word in Evangelism-in-Depth. In its simplest terms, it is an effort to mobilize every Christian believer—man, woman, child, illiterate, intellectual, new Christian and mature disciple—in an all-out witness to Jesus Christ. Too often our churches are like an Oriental sampan—it has only one oar, so one man rows hard while everyone else rides as a passenger. A better picture of the Christian church would be a racing shell, or a war canoe, with an oar in the hands of each person on board. There are no passengers in Evangelism-in-Depth—only crew members! The child may need a smaller oar, but everyone does his part!

In order to mobilize Christians it is not necessary to import great numbers of outside specialists. In fact, this may be detrimental. The job of mobilizing, if it is to produce lasting results, must be done by local leaders. The outside specialist might be able to do a better job, but he is here today and gone tomorrow. In each part of His vineyard God already has His chosen workers. They need to be called out, prayed out, and trained.

When the Evangelism-in-Depth team went to the Dominican Republic, they were told that there was insufficient leadership capability among the Dominican Christians for such a nationwide movement. So a number of foreigners and missionaries were appointed to key positions.

Then the revolution broke out, and many of the foreigners left the country. Capable or not, Dominicans had to fill the gaps. God moved among them, helping them to rise to the occasion in a way that brought glory to His name.

Our responsibility, then, is to discover all the resources which have been placed at our disposal—men, money, methods, means of all sorts—and to see that they are pooled and placed in the Master's hands. This is the proper preparation for the evangelistic miracle.

Experience has shown that when Christians sow the seed abundantly, when they work together, when they pool all their resources—few though they may be—God can use this dedicated minority to make an impact on an entire nation. In fact, this has always been God's way of doing things. He prefers not to work by many but by few. He sent home the excess warriors of Gideon's army and used only a select band of three hundred, lest sinful men be tempted to take the credit for the victory.

David alone, when in God's will, could destroy a giant. Jonathan needed only his armor-bearer when he went to battle in God's name. Throughout the history of Israel it was always the valiant few who emerged victorious when God fought their battles for them. It took only a few Spirit-filled disciples to turn the world upside down and to spread the gospel of Christ across the hostile Roman Empire.

This attitude of faith and boldness, of courage and confidence, of aggressiveness and persistence, of joyful trust and expectation, is the essential ingredient of effective and fruitful victory in Evangelism-in-Depth. Through its yearlong program of activities, Christians are challenged to enter into the apostolic attitude of Acts 4, where after the disciples had prayed, the Holy Spirit came upon them and they "spake with boldness" the word which had been committed to them.

Through prayer cells, in the training classes, and in the activities that mark a nation's special year of in-depth evangelism, believers are consistently challenged to let the Holy Spirit nurture in their hearts an evangelical enthusiasm that makes them effective witnesses for their Lord and Saviour. Through the example of other Christians, in the fellowship of prayer and in the study of God's Word, fires of evangelistic vision and holy enthusiasm are transmitted by natural contagion and by supernatural inspiration throughout the rank and file of the Christian church.

Prayer is the atmosphere of mobilization. When our Lord wanted to burden His disciples for the unreached harvests He said to them, "Pray therefore the Lord of the harvest to send out laborers into his harvest" (Matt. 9:38, RSV). As they prayed, their own vision was enlarged and their own hearts were opened, with the result that in the following chapter we discover that they themselves were the workers to be sent out!

Therefore, during the first months of an Evangelism-in-Depth movement the primary emphasis is on prayer, with the formation of cell groups to carry on throughout the entire effort, the celebration of all-night prayer vigils and other meetings. In this atmosphere of prayer, the Holy Spirit can and does burden Christians for their unsaved friends and relatives, and makes it easier to witness to them. In this atmosphere, pastors and lay Christians rededicate themselves to Christ, realigning their relationships, establishing new Christ-centered priorities, and offering themselves for Christian service. As they pray, the Holy Spirit motivates them for evangelism, and they become ready for meaningful and large-scale involvement in the yearlong program of in-depth witness.

If mobilization is the first secret of Evangelism-in-Depth, its second distinctive dimension is found in its relationship to the church, because Christians can be effectively mobilized only within the framework of the church. This means taking into account the church at its local level; it means working in and through the denomination or family of churches; and it also means mobilizing God's people together in the totality of the evangelical community, or the body of Christ, in the given nation or place.

103

The local church is extremely **important** for the spiritual nurture of any Christian, particularly that of the new believer. The epistle to the Hebrews has good reason for exhorting us not to neglect the "gathering together" of ourselves. Every child needs a family in which to mature, in which to learn to live with other people of varying ages, temperaments and relationships. To the new believer the church is his family.

The church is also the school in which he learns the deep things of God, the disciplines of life and the spiritual secrets of the Christian faith. To use still another figure, the local church is for the new believer the team on which he will be playing, the task force in which he must do his part for the spread of the gospel.

Because of the local church's inestimable importance to each Christian, Evangelism-in-Depth seeks to relate its program dynamically to the local church. It is in the church that the prayer cells are organized. The pastor of the church teaches the training classes. In the framework of the church the visitation program is structured and carried out. Evangelistic campaigns and many other activities are centered in the local congregation.

It is not always easy to communicate this perspective to the pastor and his flock. Other traditions are deep-seated, and for Evangelism-in-Depth to take hold in a church, frequently a spiritual revolution must be effected.

Perhaps the church has been pastor-centered, with the pulpit as its axis instead of the pew. If so, the position must be reversed.

Perhaps the patterns of church activity need to be changed from a "come" structure to a "go" structure.

So often **the burden of the pastor's** exhortation is to come to church. All activities are centered within the four walls of the church building. Even the unbeliever if he is to hear the gospel must come to the church to hear it. It almost seems as though the Great Commission has been reversed to read: "Come ye from all the world to hear the gospel."

This pattern must change! The church needs a revolution!

Instead of serving as a corral into which unbelievers must somehow be enticed or driven, it must become a center from which the people and the message go out to touch every needy area of the community and of the world. No other pattern is scriptural. Christians are supposed to be the "salt of the earth." But the salt is stockpiled! The church has become a warehouse. Let it serve rather as a salt refinery, sending its product into a needy world. The local church, properly oriented, is the key to effectiveness in evangelism.

Evangelism-in-Depth seeks to work within the framework of the church on the denominational level as well. In a very real sense, it is a movement of the denominations. In Latin America, the advisory team of the Latin America Mission will consent to move into a country only when the invitation to do so is extended by a representative national committee and is specifically endorsed by each of the participating groups and denominations. This denominational endorsement must carry with it a commitment to put personnel and funds at the disposal of the national committee. Above all, it must imply the intention of setting aside denominational programs for the period of Evangelism-in-Depth and making the latter its own official evangelistic activity for that time.

The leaders of Evangelism-in-Depth sit down with denominational officers before the movement gets under way to try to help them to understand how they can best take advantage of the spiritual momentum and evangelistic dynamic that will, by God's grace, be generated. Retreats are held for the pastors and workers of each denomination to help them plan their strategy. Again, halfway through the yearlong effort the denominational leaders are encouraged to seek from God a plan for continuation and projection of the evangelistic goals beyond the time allotted for the cooperative Evangelism-in-Depth movement.

The reason for this emphasis on the denominational level is clear. Usually it is from the denominational offices that the strategic planning for the work of the church emanates. This is the level on which programs of stewardship, of Christian education, of leadership training, of missions and of evangelism are evolved. The surest and best way of making Evangelism-in-Depth effective is to guarantee that the cooperating denominations properly anticipate its potential and capitalize on its momentum to pursue their own denominational goals of growth and expansion.

Yet we cannot stop there. To mobilize Christians within the framework of the local church and of their denomination would be fulfilling only part of our responsibility. This mobilization must be carried on also within the framework of the total Christian community, of the complete body of Christ in the area concerned—of the church at large. This too is a part of the evangelistic responsibility.

How can a non-Christian be expected to understand a gospel that is preached in a multitude of different places with different accents and emphases and in conflicting contexts? To him the Presbyterians, the Baptists, the Methodists and the Pentecostals are all offering their own brands of religion, and he is not challenged by their cacophony. "If the trumpet give an uncertain sound, who shall prepare himself to the battle?" (I Cor. 14:8).

Because God's Word enjoins unity in evangelical testimony, and because Christ Himself prayed that His disciples might be one in order that the world might believe, Evangelism-in-Depth structures its program so that on several occasions during the course of the year Christians of all denominations will have opportunity to proclaim together their common faith and their single Saviour. It may be in massive parades, in pastors' retreats, in youth rallies, or in joint evangelistic services. Without compromising their respective denominational distinctives, the Christians who are joined in Evangelism-in-Depth find deep satisfaction and spiritual joy in proclaiming by their very presence together the one Lord, the one faith, the one gospel, the one Name under heaven whereby men must be saved.

A third distinctive principle of Evangelism-in-Depth refers to the leadership upon which the mobilization of all Christians in witness must depend. If the movement is not to be something that is here today and gone tomorrow, *its leadership must be local.* The church cannot be mobilized by foreigners and imported leaders, but only by those leaders who are a part of the ongoing picture and pattern of the church.

The fact of the matter is that in every part of the vineyard God already has His workers who need only to be discovered, challenged and motivated. In potential the leadership is there.

Evangelism-in-Depth invariably turns up some previously unsuspected leadership talent. There are so many activities and opportunities to exercise leadership that if a man shows promise on one level he can be quickly moved up to another one. While in normal times the process of leadership training is something like one or two men trying to climb a ladder, during Evangelism-in-Depth it is more like a pyramid with people constantly swarming up all its sides. Working from such a broad base and with so much opportunity, leadership potential is developed very rapidly. Whether it be in the local area, on the denominational level, or on the national level, new leadership is constantly emerging.

The sovereign Spirit of God often anoints for special tasks people whom we would not expect to respond in this way. Acknowledged leaders are frequently too busy about other things, and so the challenge and the burden fall on untrained shoulders. This too is part of God's plan, and we need to learn to follow rather than to anticipate the Spirit's activity. Wherever this is done, God will never lack for local leadership to mobilize His people in the framework of the church for effective Christian witness.

It was the growing understanding of this premise more than anything else that moved the Latin America Mission to shift the emphasis of its contribution in Evangelism-in-Depth efforts from a *coordination* of such efforts to the role of *technical assistance* and

108

counseling in their coordination. Therefore, members of the LAM task force are called "advisers" rather than "coordinators." It is the local leadership of the evangelical church that must plan and implement each program of Evangelism-in-Depth.

The final principle of in-depth evangelism is wrapped up in what we might call a global or comprehensive objective. As we try to implement our Lord's Great Commission in terms of today, we suddenly become conscious of the fact that we have been very provincial and individualistic in our response to His command. Christ told us to disciple all the nations, and instead of trying to find ways of truly evangelizing, Christianizing, or discipling a nation, we have been content to think in terms of winning a few disciples from each nation, as if this were in itself the fulfillment of the Great Commission.

In our days of denominational separatism and of individualistic missionary activity, we have to some degree lost sight of the goal of winning an entire nation for Jesus Christ. Whole classes of people and whole societies have been neglected. We have failed to study our objectives systematically, to look at our target areas wholly, and to pool our resources for a total impact on a nation for Jesus Christ.

If any concept reverberates through the Great Commission as it is expressed and reexpressed in the four Gospels and in Acts, it is the concept of totality. "*All* power is given unto me in heaven and in earth" (Matt. 28:18); "Go ye into *all* the world and preach the gospel" (Mark 16:15); "Disciple *all* nations, . . . teaching them . . . *all* things whatsoever I have commanded you: and, lo, I am with you alway, [*all* the days,

109

Amplified] even unto the end of the world" (Matt. 28:19-20, marginal).

Surely the words of Christ require us to think in large, bold terms. Certainly they enjoin us to pool our resources in a coordinated plan of activity that will give hope of accomplishing His purpose. Obviously our evangelistic preaching must be accompanied by profound and far-reaching exposition that will communicate the whole counsel of God and bring the gospel to bear on the whole of man's life. It is the Saviour's purpose that the gospel should reach each man and then change, motivate and activate him in all his social, political and economic structures, as well as in each of his relationships in the home, the school, the shop, the village, the office, the province, the nation and the world.

Very frankly, we can see no other way of getting the job done. However, if by God's grace all Christians can be mobilized in effective witness within the framework of the church and by their own local leaders, with these broad objectives in view, then certainly the evangelistic task of the church is not beyond fulfillment and the Great Commission of Jesus Christ can be carried out before He comes. It may require a revolution in the church, but it can be done.

In a day of general pessimism and in the face of a floodtide of secular forces, we believe Christ's promise is still true. When His will becomes ours, and His Word is applied to our hearts and in His church, the very gates of hell cannot prevail against us.

10

RIGHT SIDE UP—
EVANGELISM-IN-DEPTH
PROGRAM

BOLIVIA has had more political revolutions than years of history, but during the first eleven months of 1965 it experienced a spiritual revolution-in-depth that turned the evangelical church right side up and the country upside down.

Perhaps it was this very disposition to change—a readiness to accept a new challenge—that made Bolivia a likely proving ground for in-depth concepts. Certainly the 1965 evangelistic effort gave them their fullest expression to that time. The program of Evangelism-in-Depth in Bolivia was well rounded and balanced.

Less than 2 percent of the Andean nation of four million people are evangelicals. Hardly an auspicious starting point! But they had the faith to believe that by coordinating their Christian witness in a yearlong Evangelism-in-Depth movement, they could together reap a harvest of souls and make a strong impact for God on their picturesque and needy land.

That they succeeded is evidenced in the marked growth of the 750 cooperating churches during the year, in the nearly 20,000 professions of faith in Christ, and in the wide coverage given to the movement—particularly to the closing campaign and dramatic parade—by all the leading dailies in La Paz, Bolivia's capital.

Bolivia is in many ways an incredible country. More than two-thirds of its population is composed of Indians who have been used and abused since colonial times, with little concern until recently for their education and the improvement of their lot. As a result, the percentage of illiteracy in Bolivia remains at 68 percent. Malnutrition is rife. Poverty is desperate. Even the pockets of prosperity seem shabby, progress slow, and politics precarious.

Nevertheless, God has been at work. Missionaries and pastors have been faithful. In recent years there has been spontaneous church growth, especially among the Altiplano (highland) Indians. Christians have been addressing themselves to their task with new enthusiasm.

On Sunday morning, November 21, fifteen thousand evangelicals in La Paz took their witness to the streets. It was an impressive sight. It took them two hours and twenty minutes to stream past a single point along the parade route. The sun was brilliant and burned through the thin mountain air, etching sharp shadows on the cobblestone streets. For hours, groups of Bolivian Christians, floats and bands had been converging on the plaza that was the parade's mustering place. At ten-thirty—right on schedule—they got under way.

I stood on a truck and watched them march past.

After the motorcycle escort came the national committee of Evangelism-in-Depth, followed by the uniformed choir. Next marched the university students and what seemed an endless succession of well-dressed businessmen, ragged farmers and tiny school children. Most colorful were the Indian women, their babies slung across their backs in brightly colored shawls, their brown-felt derbies planted securely above their round Indian faces. Equally impressive were the tin miners with helmets and goggles, the typical peasant bands, and the colorful floats. The parade was a precedent-shattering experience for evangelicals in the capital city of a nation that had been experiencing precedent-shattering events all through the year.

Twenty-two men from Oruro had cycled two hundred fifty kilometers to parade in La Paz. A total of fifteen hundred came from Oruro, almost as many from Cochabamba. From all over the country—by truck, train, bus, car, plane—they crowded into La Paz, overtaxing every hospitality arrangement, sleeping on church benches or even, in some cases, on the ground outside. They were all on hand Sunday morning, however, joyously ready to march for Jesus Christ.

They paraded in perfect order, many of them with portable radios tuned to the evangelical station, The Southern Cross. From remote-control posts along the route the station was broadcasting instructions and leading the great crowd in songs and choruses as they marched. It was unforgettable.

One Indian, who as the first believer in his village had suffered much persecution, was awed by the magnitude of the public witness. "I never knew I had so many brothers," he exclaimed.

In an open letter to the nation's Protestants, *Presencia*, the Roman Catholic newspaper, said:

> You have completed a series of activities which was crowned yesterday with a great manifestation that moved through the city before the astonished eyes of many spectators. It was a manifestation that pleased us greatly. . . .
>
> The diverse Protestant sects have united here and have organized these activities in spite of their differences, with the Gospel as a backdrop. . . .

The Catholic commentator, who simply signed his name "Xavier," went on to point out that the parade was notable both for its magnitude and for the humility and lack of pomp by which it was characterized. "Both of these things pleased me," he said. "The people paraded with serenity, in good order, and with conviction reflected on their faces."

The fact that the evangelicals were clean, nicely dressed, and without the marks of alcohol on their faces was proof to *Presencia* of "a social action and of a philosophy of preaching which produces positive results for these people and for the nation."

Evangelism-in-Depth's concluding weeks in the world's highest capital city were exciting, both spiritually and otherwise. Despite several days of cold rain, evening meetings in the unroofed coliseum were well attended, the crowd growing to ten thousand at the last Saturday night service. Argentine evangelist, Santiago Garabaya, gave a clear gospel message to which more than one thousand Bolivians responded by confessing faith in Jesus Christ. Tenor Jesse

Morales **from Texas** was the popular soloist for the series.

Publicity for the crusade was profuse. No one could remain ignorant of the Protestant witness. Both of Bolivia's copresidents were heard to comment favorably on the campaign, and one of them, President Ovando Candia, attended an Evangelism-in-Depth luncheon on Saturday, where he gave public tribute to the contribution being made by the evangelicals to the spiritual and social welfare of his country. He said:

I would like to begin my brief words to you by expressing on behalf of General Barrientos and myself our most sincere thanks for the privilege which has been extended to us to share with you the bread and salt of evangelical hospitality.

I have spoken many times in a military context and recently in political tones. In the present circumstances I would like above all to lift my thought to God, the Creator of all that exists in the universe, and ask Him that violence might be exiled from the world, that peace might reign among us, and that we might follow the sage precept of loving one another.

I would like also to recognize the immense labor of the Evangelical Church in Bolivia. It has opened the doors of culture to the humble ones of my people. It gives them a chance to struggle against sickness. It fits them too for the struggle of life. For this reason, in the name of the supreme Government, in the name of the Bolivian people, I cannot but express my most sincere thanks to those who thus contribute to the individual and collective betterment of my Fatherland.

I sincerely believe, gentlemen, that your evangelical mission, a mission of taking the Word of

115

God to all the inhabitants of the globe, is the mission of privileged men. You may well be proud of it. Not only do you contribute to the betterment of the material life of the inhabitants—in this case, of Bolivia—you are also the engineers of its soul, because matter and soul together constitute the essence of man who is made after the image of God. Thank you very much.

Behind the more spectacular events like the parade and the presidential luncheon were the yearlong labors of the Latin America Mission's team of technical advisers and of the many national, regional and functional coordinators who directed the cooperative movement. These men and women, released and supported by their respective denominations, made it possible for the gospel witness in Bolivia during 1965 to be deep as well as broad in its impact. By making substantial financial contributions and by releasing ten men full time for coordination, Bolivian denominations established a new record for cooperation and made it possible to decentralize the administration of Evangelism-in-Depth while at the same time assuring the coordinated advance of the movement across the nation.

These coordinators organized 4,204 prayer cells and many all-night prayer vigils. They instructed pastors how to carry on training classes in their own churches to prepare not just a few but all believers for evangelistic witness. They organized visitation programs, systematically covering every city block and country hamlet.

It was estimated that eighteen thousand people participated in the visitation program. As in Venezuela, it was linked very closely to the local campaigns sponsored in each of the cooperating churches. Once more the visitation proved to be the most fruitful phase in the Evangelism-in-Depth movement.

Because of Bolivia's evident physical and material needs, Evangelism-in-Depth very naturally found abundant ways in which to express, within a framework not of philanthropy but of evangelism, the social concern of the Protestant community. With the cooperation of ALFALIT, a literacy agency, hundreds of teachers were prepared and thousands of adults were enabled for the first time to read portions of God's Word.

A program of approximately thirty Goodwill Caravans took the services of doctors, dentists, nurses, agronomists, and literacy experts to remote and underprivileged areas of the country. An American dentist and his nurse-wife journeyed from the United States at their own expense to participate in some of these much-appreciated caravans. Three caravans near La Paz, for example, reported 233 patients given medical care, 176 extractions by the dentist and 27 conversions to the Christian faith.

Evangelism-in-Depth was concerned with reaching not only the underprivileged. Students in Bolivia's seven universities were the target of special activities carried on by the evangelical student groups and capped by popular lectures given by Gerardo de Avila, a Cuban member of the LAM team. De Avila ably communicated the pure gospel message to modern students in their own context and thought forms.

From Puerto Rico came Mrs. Aimee de Cortese, renowned evangelist, for a successful series of campaigns for women. Youth and children's rallies provided youngsters with **opportunities for Christian** service and witness. Bible knowledge contests were held in youth groups everywhere.

Advisers and coordinators crisscrossed the nation, planning, mobilizing, preaching and training. One of the Latin America Mission's team of advisers, Charles Koch, reported on a typical visit to the rough jungle department of the Beni. After a hair-raising flight of an hour and a half in a DC-3 from Cochabamba, Koch was met at Trinidad by the local coordinator. He described his subsequent experiences in a letter:

> Within minutes after my arrival in Trinidad, I climbed into the small, single-engine plane of one of the missionary workers of the Bolivian Indian Mission. We flew for about an hour to the city of Magdalena, and the next day, another forty minutes to the city of Santa Ana. In each of these stops we presented the film, *Lucia*.
>
> The following day I boarded a commercial DC-3 flight and after an hour and a half, arrived in Guayaramarine. At the home of some Christians I met a woman who told me this story:
>
> "Evangelism-in-Depth has been a wonderful thing for me and for our church. Before, we thought that the job of witnessing was in the hands of our pastor. My husband was converted a short time ago, although I have been a Christian for quite a while. . . ."
>
> She continued, "We listen to the radio program, *Llamada a la Oración* [Call to Prayer], every day so we know exactly what is going on in Evangelism-in-Depth all over the country. [In these areas, the publication *En Marcha* arrives about two months late because of the poor mail service.] I will never forget May 7, National Visitation Day for Evangelism-in-Depth. We went out to visit. I went with fear. I didn't know what

118

they would say. Tears of joy ran down my face that day because eight persons of those that I visited gave their hearts to the Lord. Now we have new courage."

Believers like this one sponsored public evangelistic campaigns in each local church and cooperative campaigns where there were several churches which joined forces. They encouraged special efforts to reach children, women, students, young people.

One young woman started a sort of revivial in her church by coming back from a youth conference and reporting that "they" had told her that every young people's society should be holding street meetings and witnessing to their faith in Jesus Christ. Since her church had no young people's society, she herself with her younger brother went out and held impromptu street meetings. They held ninety of them!

The program of Evangelism-in-Depth in Bolivia was built around the same six basic elements which have formed the backbone of each of the national experiments in Latin America. They are not new or startling; the same elements are common to the evangelistic experience of the church everywhere. They include prayer, training, visitation, special activities, evangelistic meetings, and consolidation or follow-through.

Certainly there is nothing revolutionary here, one is tempted to say. The distinctive thing about these phases of Evangelism-in-Depth, however, is the way in which they can be structured to implement the in-depth principles.

For example, prayer cells are not new, but to organize them in a nationwide attempt to include every

119

Christian in every church, and to use them as means for seeking revival, motivation and power in evangelistic witness is less common. In Bolivia twenty thousand adults and young people were meeting regularly to pray for their unsaved friends and neighbors. They launched each new phase of the movement with all-night or half-night prayer vigils in the local churches. In doing so, they opened their hearts for an inward working of God's Spirit that made them clear channels and fruitful agents of Christian witness throughout the length and breadth of the land.

Often the cells themselves were the scenes of conversion. In the Dominican Republic, where 732 persons were reported to have accepted Christ in the prayer cells alone, adviser Miguel Suazo discovered one congregation of fifteen members that had reported the formation of sixteen cells! This seemed strange, so Suazo investigated and found out that some of the Christians were meeting each day in the homes of different unconverted friends to pray with them for Evangelism-in-Depth and its impact on their community. It is not hard to believe that Suazo discovered forty-five people who had accepted Christ as their Saviour through this unique ministry of prayer and witness!

The training program poses other opportunities for the application of in-depth principles. There are in existence many lay-training programs. Most of them are aimed at specific—usually more mature—groups of Christians. The training program of Evangelism-in-Depth, however, is geared to the elementary understanding of all believers and is intended to equip not only the church deacon but also the illiterate new believer, and even the child, for his life of testimony before a needy world.

To accomplish its purpose, the weekly training class must be given at a time when the greatest part of the congregation is in attendance. In Latin America, if the classes are given on Saturday night they would perhaps catch the young people in church. Monday night might be fine for the faithful women. But if the pastor really intends to train his congregation he will probably have to give the class on Sunday morning, or whenever he can get the most members of his flock together.

Note that it is the pastor who teaches the lesson. The shepherd must go before his sheep. The mobilization must be carried out by local leadership. The pastor cannot be short-circuited if the local church is to experience enduring revival.

This is also true for the program of house-to-house visitation. Each church is made responsible for a specific section of the town or city, and the entire program of visitation is executed by the pastor with his people. He leads them out in pairs, and they go not just to leave a piece of literature or to extend an invitation to a meeting, but rather with the purpose and adequate training to make each encounter an opportunity to present the claims of the gospel.

Step by step, in all of its special activities as well as in its evangelistic meetings—local, regional, or capital city campaigns—the Evangelism-in-Depth program is a conscientious effort not only to preach the gospel by every means, but to involve every Christian in the evangelistic task. This was the constant thrust of the team's efforts in Bolivia: to revive and motivate the

Christian church, its leadership and membership, on every level of organization, in a full-orbed witness to the saving grace and transforming power of Christ. The presence of the church, in every structure and relationship of Bolivian society, was felt as never before, and the church's ministry and witness attained new dimensions of outreach and quality.

The Latin America Mission's team of advisers was headed by Rafael Baltodano, a dynamic Nicaraguan with experience in three previous Evangelism-in-Depth movements. One of the most far-reaching and significant contributions the team made to the work in Bolivia was to help the denominations line up their objectives and their advance programs for the consolidation of results. They were helped to realize how they might put to work their newly acquired skills during the months ahead.

Fourteen of the major denominations in Bolivia met in short retreats with LAM adviser Burnis Bushong, on loan from the World Gospel Mission. At these gatherings, plans were laid for follow-up evangelistic efforts, and as the formal campaign was ended, the denominations moved in at once with their own program of consolidation and advance.

In short, the advisers and the coordinators helped the evangelical church in Bolivia develop from a centripetal attitude ("come to every meeting") to a centrifugal one ("go witness for Jesus Christ"). They helped the church move from a pastor-centered program of exhortation to a people-centered program of participation. They shifted the focus from pulpit to pew. They were the Holy Spirit's agents for bringing a spiritual revolution to the community.

With God's help, they turned the program of the Christian church right side up and, in so doing, could be said to have turned Bolivia upside down. Like their brethren in the Dominican Republic, Venezuela, Guatemala and elsewhere, the Bolivian Christians simply became involved in a spiritual revolution.

EPILOGUE

"EXCUSE, PLEASE!"

From the front row of the balcony the Japanese evangelist rose to speak, his Taiwanese interpreter at his side.

The debate had been getting warm, as delegates to the August, 1966, Continental Institute of Evangelism-in-Depth in Costa Rica were discussing some minor problems of relationship encountered in South America. The interchange was being carried on in Spanish, with simultaneous translation into English for those in the balcony wearing headphones.

For Koji Honda to understand what was going on, Bill Lee, who was proficient in English and Japanese, had to whisper in his ear. Now Evangelist Honda, his stocky frame vibrant with enthusiasm, stood to address the congress by double interpretation.

"As an evangelist in Japan," he began, "I have learned that Christians can work together when they want to. We belong to the same God; we believe the same Bible; we preach the same Gospel of Jesus Christ; and we expect the same Holy Spirit to convert sinners to repentance. This is all we need! Let's get together and get on with the job!"

By the time the Japanese had been translated into English by a Chinese and then into Spanish by a Panamanian, the brief speech had become a three-ring circus! Mr. Honda was obviously enjoying himself, and his enthusiasm made his message even more convincing. It was this as much as his words that won the crowd's immediate sympathy. He was applauded, and the discussion continued—but no longer was it ridden by tensions. It was characterized instead by happy good fellowship.

The Japanese evangelist's contribution also symbolized the spirit and character of the institute. It was basically Latin American, but it had worldwide repercussions. Originally planned for the purpose of training coordinators for the forthcoming Evangelism-in-Depth movements in Peru and Colombia, the workshop had grown unexpectedly as leaders from an ever increasing number of countries heard about it, became interested, and asked to attend. By the time the two weeks of sessions were ready to start, some one hundred fifty pastors, workers and missionaries from other Latin American countries were on hand at the Biblical Seminary in San José, Costa Rica. This number did not include the scores of Costa Ricans, fifty or so seminarians, plus local missionaries, language school students and others.

The most surprising area of escalation in attendance was in the number of delegates who arrived from outside Latin America—two from Japan, three from Taiwan, two from Nigeria, one from the Congo, two from the non-Spanish-speaking islands of the West Indies, twelve from the Kentucky mountain area of Appalachia, and another dozen from other parts of the United States. Their contribution to the discussions was timely and appreciated.

In fact, so many non-Spanish-speaking delegates arrived that it became impractical to rely entirely upon simultaneous translation, and during most of the daytime hours two simultaneous institutes were conducted —one in Spanish and one in English.

The dichotomy of the program was definitely symbolic. It sharply pointed up the worldwide interest in the application of in-depth principles of evangelism. Not only were Evangelism-in-Depth movements planned in Latin America—Peru in 1967 and Colombia in 1968—but outside Latin America as well. Nigeria was moving into its third year of "New Life for All." The Congo was about to launch its "Christ for All" campaign. The Republic of Free China on the island of Taiwan was anticipating a three-year Evangelism-in-Depth movement to mobilize the entire Protestant community in a soul-winning outreach.

Discussions at the workshop sessions in August were practical as well as inspiring. The Spirit of God was at work in the minds and hearts of His people. Rubén Lores summed things up: "Evangelism-in-Depth is a movement, not a monument. It can properly be called a 'phenomenon.' It is not something we of the Latin America Mission are developing. It is something God is doing, and we are merely privileged observers. In Latin America and around the world it is the Church of Jesus Christ, caught up in evangelistic revival. It is a spiritual revolution. And God's people are the true revolutionaries."